FOREWORD

The collection of "Everything Will Be Okay" travel phrasebooks published by T&P Books is designed for people traveling abroad for tourism and business. The phrasebooks contain what matters most - the essentials for basic communication. This is an indispensable set of phrases to "survive" while abroad.

This phrasebook will help you in most cases where you need to ask something, get directions, find out how much something costs, etc. It can also resolve difficult communication situations where gestures just won't help.

This book contains a lot of phrases that have been grouped according to the most relevant topics. A separate section of the book also provides a small dictionary with more than 1,500 important and useful words.

Take "Everything Will Be Okay" phrasebook with you on the road and you'll have an irreplaceable traveling companion who will help you find your way out of any situation and teach you to not fear speaking with foreigners.

TABLE OF CONTENTS

T&P Books Publishing

Travel phrasebooks collection
«Everything Will Be Okay!»

T&P Books Publishing

PHRASEBOOK
· LITHUANIAN ·

THE MOST IMPORTANT PHRASES

This phrasebook contains
the most important
phrases and questions
for basic communication
Everything you need
to survive overseas

By Andrey Taranov

T&P BOOKS

Phrasebook + 1500-word dictionary

English-Lithuanian phrasebook & concise dictionary

By Andrey Taranov

The collection of "Everything Will Be Okay" travel phrasebooks published by T&P Books is designed for people traveling abroad for tourism and business. The phrasebooks contain what matters most - the essentials for basic communication. This is an indispensable set of phrases to "survive" while abroad.

Another section of the book also provides a small dictionary with more than 1,500 useful words arranged alphabetically. The dictionary includes a lot of gastronomic terms and will be helpful when ordering food at a restaurant or buying groceries at the store.

T&P Books Publishing
www.tpbooks.com

ISBN: 978-1-78716-262-4

This book is also available in E-book formats.
Please visit www.tpbooks.com or the major online bookstores.

PRONUNCIATION

Letter	Lithuanian example	T&P phonetic alphabet	English example
Aa	adata	[a]	shorter than in ask
Ąą	ąžuolas	[a:]	calf, palm
Bb	badas	[b]	baby, book
Cc	cukrus	[ʦ]	cats, tsetse fly
Čč	česnakas	[ʧ]	church, French
Dd	dumblas	[d]	day, doctor
Ee	eglė	[æ]	chess, man
Ęę	vedęs	[æ:]	longer than in brand
Ėė	ėdalas	[e:]	longer than in bell
Ff	fleita	[f]	face, food
Gg	gandras	[g]	game, gold
Hh	husaras	[ɣ]	between [g] and [h]
I i	ižas	[i]	shorter than in feet
Į į	mįslė	[i:]	feet, meter
Yy	vynas	[i:]	feet, meter
J j	juokas	[j]	yes, New York
Kk	kilpa	[k]	clock, kiss
L l	laisvė	[l]	lace, people
Mm	mama	[m]	magic, milk
Nn	nauda	[n]	name, normal
Oo	ola	[o], [o:]	floor, doctor
Pp	pirtis	[p]	pencil, private
Rr	ragana	[r]	rice, radio
Ss	sostinė	[s]	city, boss
Šš	šūvis	[ʃ]	machine, shark
Tt	tėvynė	[t]	tourist, trip
Uu	upė	[u]	book
Ųų	siųsti	[u:]	pool, room
Ūū	ūmėdė	[u:]	pool, room
Vv	vabalas	[ʋ]	vase, winter
Zz	zuikis	[z]	zebra, please
Žž	žiurkė	[ʒ]	forge, pleasure

Comments

- A macron (ū), an ogonek (ą, ę, į, ų) can all be used to mark vowel length in Modern Standard Lithuanian. Acute (Áá Ą́ą́), grave (Àà), and tilde (Ãã Ą̃ą̃) diacritics are used to indicate pitch accents. However, these pitch accents are generally not written, except in dictionaries, grammars, and where needed for clarity, such as to differentiate homonyms and dialectal use.

LIST OF ABBREVIATIONS

English abbreviations

ab.	-	about
adj	-	adjective
adv	-	adverb
anim.	-	animate
as adj	-	attributive noun used as adjective
e.g.	-	for example
etc.	-	et cetera
fam.	-	familiar
fem.	-	feminine
form.	-	formal
inanim.	-	inanimate
masc.	-	masculine
math	-	mathematics
mil.	-	military
n	-	noun
pl	-	plural
pron.	-	pronoun
sb	-	somebody
sing.	-	singular
sth	-	something
v aux	-	auxiliary verb
vi	-	intransitive verb
vi, vt	-	intransitive, transitive verb
vt	-	transitive verb

Lithuanian abbreviations

dgs	-	plural
m	-	feminine noun
m dgs	-	feminine plural
v	-	masculine noun
v dgs	-	masculine plural

LITHUANIAN PHRASEBOOK

This section contains
important phrases that may
come in handy in various
real-life situations.
The phrasebook will help
you ask for directions, clarify
a price, buy tickets, and
order food at a restaurant

T&P Books Publishing

PHRASEBOOK
CONTENTS

T&P Books Publishing

Excuse me, ...	**Atsiprašau, ...** [atsʲɪpra'ʃɑʊ, ...]
Hello.	**Sveikì.** [svʲɛɪ'kʲɪ.]
Thank you.	**Ãčiū.** ['a:tsʲu:.]
Good bye.	**Ikì.** [ɪ'kʲɪ.]
Yes.	**Taĩp.** ['tʌɪp.]
No.	**Nè.** ['nʲɛ.]
I don't know.	**Nežinaũ.** [nʲɛʒʲɪ'nɑʊ.]
Where? | Where to? | When?	**Kur̃? | Kur? | Kadà?** ['kʊr? | 'kʊr? | ka'da?]

I need ...	**Mán reĩkia ...** ['man 'rʲɛɪkʲɛ ...]
I want ...	**Nóriu ...** ['norʲʊ ...]
Do you have ...?	**Ar̃ tùrite ...?** [ar 'tʊrʲɪtʲɛ ...?]
Is there a ... here?	**Ar̃ čià yrà ...?** [ar 'tsʲæ i:'ra ...?]
May I ...?	**Ar̃ galiù ...?** [ar ga'lʲʊ ...?]
..., please (polite request)	**Prašaũ ...** [pra'ʃɑʊ ...]

I'm looking for ...	**Íeškau ...** ['ɪʲɛʃkɑʊ ...]
restroom	**tualèto** [tʊa'lʲɛtɔ]
ATM	**bankomãto** [baŋko'ma:tɔ]
pharmacy (drugstore)	**vaĩstinės** ['vʌɪstʲɪnʲe:s]
hospital	**ligóninės** [lʲɪ'gonʲɪnʲe:s]
police station	**polìcijos sky̆riaus** [po'lʲɪtsɪjos 'skʲi:rʲɛʊs]
subway	**metrò** [mʲɛ'tro]

taxi	**taksi** [tak's⁞ɪ]
train station	**traukinių stotiẽs** [traʊkˈɪˈnʲu: sto'tʲɛs]

My name is ...	**Mãno var̃das ...** ['ma:nɔ 'vardas ...]
What's your name?	**Kuõ jũs vardù?** ['kʊɑ 'ju:s var'dʊ?]
Could you please help me?	**Atsiprašaũ, ar̃ gãlite padéti?** [atsˈɪpra'ʃaʊ, ar 'ga:lʲɪte pa'dʲe:tʲɪ?]
I've got a problem.	**Atsitiko problemà.** [atsʲɪ'tʲɪkɔ problʲɛ'ma.]
I don't feel well.	**Mán blogà.** ['man blʲo'ga.]
Call an ambulance!	**Kviẽskite greĩtąją!** ['kvʲɛskʲɪtʲɛ 'grʲɛɪta:ja:!]
May I make a call?	**Ar̃ galiù paskam̃binti?** [ar ga'lʲʊ pas'kambʲɪntʲɪ?]

I'm sorry.	**Atsiprašaũ.** [atsʲɪpra'ʃaʊ.]
You're welcome.	**Nėrà už kã.** [nʲe:'ra 'ʊʒ ka:.]

I, me	**àš** ['aʃ]
you (inform.)	**tù** ['tʊ]
he	**jìs** [jɪs]
she	**jì** [jɪ]
they (masc.)	**jiẽ** ['jiɛ]
they (fem.)	**jõs** ['jɔ:s]
we	**mẽs** ['mʲæs]
you (pl)	**jũs** ['ju:s]
you (sg, form.)	**Jũs** ['ju:s]

ENTRANCE	**ĮÉJIMAS** [iː'ɛː'jɪmas]
EXIT	**IŠÉJIMAS** [ɪʃ'e:'jɪmas]
OUT OF ORDER	**NEVEĨKIA** [nʲɛ'vʲɛɪkʲɛ]
CLOSED	**UŽDARÝTA** [ʊʒda'rʲiː:ta]

OPEN	**ATIDARYTA** [atˈɪdaˈrʲiːta]
FOR WOMEN	**MÓTERŲ** [ˈmotʲɛruː]
FOR MEN	**VYRŲ** [ˈvʲiːruː]

Questions

Where?	**Kur̃?** ['kʊr?]
Where to?	**Į̃ kur̃?** [iː 'kʊr?]
Where from?	**Ìš kur̃?** [ɪʃ 'kʊr?]
Why?	**Kodė̃l?** [kɔ'dʲeːlʲ?]
For what reason?	**Kodė̃l?** [kɔ'dʲeːlʲ?]
When?	**Kadà?** [ka'da?]
How long?	**Kíek laĩko?** ['kʲiɛk 'lʲʌɪko?]
At what time?	**Kadà?** [ka'da?]
How much?	**Kíek?** ['kʲiɛk?]
Do you have …?	**Ar̃ tùrite …?** [ar 'tʊrʲɪtʲɛ …?]
Where is …?	**Kur̃ yrà …?** ['kʊr iː'ra …?]
What time is it?	**Kíek dabar̃ valandų̃?** ['kʲiɛk da'bar valʲan'duː?]
May I make a call?	**Ar̃ galiù paskam̃binti?** [ar ga'lʲʊ pas'kambʲɪntʲɪ?]
Who's there?	**Kàs teñ?** ['kas tʲɛn?]
Can I smoke here?	**Ar̃ čià galimà rūkýti?** [ar 'tʂʲæ galʲɪ'ma ruː'kʲiːtʲɪ?]
May I …?	**Ar̃ galiù …?** [ar ga'lʲʊ …?]

Needs

I'd like ...	**Noréčiau ...** [no'rʲɐ:tʂʲɛʊ ...]
I don't want ...	**Nenóriu ...** [nʲɛ'norʲʊ ...]
I'm thirsty.	**Nóriu atsigérti.** ['norʲʊ atsʲɪ'gʲɛrtʲɪ.]
I want to sleep.	**Nóriu miẽgo.** ['norʲʊ 'mʲɛgɔ.]

I want ...	**Nóriu ...** ['norʲʊ ...]
to wash up	**nusipraũsti** [nʊsʲɪ'praʊstʲɪ]
to brush my teeth	**išsivalýti dantìs** [ɪʃsʲɪva'lʲi:tʲɪ dan'tʲɪs]
to rest a while	**trupùtį pailséti** [trʊ'pʊtʲɪ: pʌɪlʲ'sʲɛ:tʲɪ]
to change my clothes	**pérsirengti** ['pʲɛrsʲɪrʲɛŋktʲɪ]

to go back to the hotel	**grįžti i viešbutį** ['grʲi:ʒtʲɪ ɪ 'vʲɛʃbʊtʲi:]
to buy ...	**nusipírkti ...** [nʊsʲɪ'pʲɪrktʲɪ ...]
to go to ...	**eĩti į̃ ...** ['ɛɪtʲɪ i: ...]
to visit ...	**aplankýti ...** [aplʲaŋ'kʲi:tʲɪ ...]
to meet with ...	**susitìkti sù ...** [sʊsʲɪ'tʲɪktʲɪ 'sʊ ...]
to make a call	**paskambìnti** [pas'kambʲɪntʲɪ]

I'm tired.	**Àš pavar̃gęs /pavar̃gusi/.** ['aʃ pa'vargʲɛ:s /pa'vargʊsʲɪ/.]
We are tired.	**Mẽs pavar̃gome.** ['mʲæs pa'vargomʲɛ.]
I'm cold.	**Mán šálta.** ['man 'ʃalʲta.]
I'm hot.	**Mán karštà.** ['man karʃta.]
I'm OK.	**Mán vìskas geraĩ.** ['man 'vʲɪskas gʲɛ'rʌɪ.]

I need to make a call.

Mán reĩkia paskam̃binti.
['man 'rʲɛɪkʲɛ pas'kambʲɪntʲɪ.]

I need to go to the restroom.

Mán reĩkia į̃ tualẽtą.
['man rʲɛɪkʲɛ iː tʊa'lʲɛta:.]

I have to go.

Mán reĩkia eĩti.
['man 'rʲɛɪkʲɛ 'ɛɪtʲɪ.]

I have to go now.

Mán jaũ reĩkia eĩti.
['man jɛʊ 'rʲɛɪkʲɛ 'ɛɪtʲɪ.]

Asking for directions

Excuse me, ...
Atsiprašaū, ...
[atsʲɪpraˈʃɑʊ, ...]

Where is ...?
Kur̃ yrà ...?
[ˈkʊr iːˈra ...?]

Which way is ...?
Į̃ kurią̃ pùsę yrà ...?
[iː kʊˈrʲæ: ˈpʊsʲɛ: iːˈra ...?]

Could you help me, please?
Atsiprašaū, ar̃ gãlite padéti?
[atsʲɪpraˈʃɑʊ, ar ˈgaːlʲɪte paˈdʲeːtʲɪ?]

I'm looking for ...
Àš íeškau ...
[ˈaʃ ˈrʲɛʃkɑʊ ...]

I'm looking for the exit.
Àš íeškau išėjìmo.
[ˈaʃ ˈɪɛʃkɑʊ iʃʲeːˈjɪmɔ.]

I'm going to ...
Àš einù į̃ ...
[ˈaʃ ɛɪˈnʊ iː ...]

Am I going the right way to ...?
Ar̃ àš teisìngai einù į̃ ...?
[ar ˈaʃ tʲɛɪˈsʲɪːŋɡʌɪ ɛɪˈnʊ iː ...?]

Is it far?
Ar̃ tolì?
[ar toˈlʲɪ?]

Can I get there on foot?
Ar̃ galiù nueĩti teñ pėsčiomìs?
[ar gaˈlʲʊ ˈnʊʲɛɪtʲɪ ten pʲeːstʃʲoˈmʲɪs?]

Can you show me on the map?
Ar̃ gãlite parodyti žemėlapyje?
[ar ˈgaːlʲɪte paˈrodʲiːtʲɪ ʒeˈmʲeːlapʲiːje?]

Show me where we are right now.
Parodykite, kur̃ dabar̃ ēsame.
[paˈrodʲiːkʲɪtʲɛ, kʊr daˈbar ˈɛsamʲɛ.]

Here
Čià
[ˈtʂʲæ]

There
Teñ
[ˈtʲɛn]

This way
Eimė̃ čià
[ɛɪˈmʲɛ tʂʲæ]

Turn right.
Sùkite dešinėñ.
[ˈsʊkʲɪte deʃɪˈnʲeːn.]

Turn left.
Sùkite kairėñ.
[ˈsʊkʲɪte kʌɪˈrʲeːn.]

first (second, third) turn
pìrmas (añtras, trẽčias) posūkis
[ˈpʲɪrmas (ˈantras, ˈtrʲeːtʃʲɛs) ˈposuːkʲɪs]

to the right	**į dešinę** [i: 'dʲæʃɪnʲɛ:]
to the left	**į kairę** [i: 'kʌɪrʲɛ:]
Go straight ahead.	**Eikite tiesiai.** ['ɛɪkʲɪtʲɛ 'tʲɛsʲɛɪ.]

Signs

WELCOME!	**SVEIKÌ ATVÝKĘ!** [sv'ɛɪ'k'ɪ at'v'i:k'ɛ:ǁ]
ENTRANCE	**ĮĖJÌMAS** [i:'ɛ:'jɪmas]
EXIT	**IŠĖJÌMAS** [ɪʃe:'jɪmas]
PUSH	**STÙMTI** ['stʊmt'ɪ]
PULL	**TRAÚKTI** ['trɑʊkt'ɪ]
OPEN	**ATIDARÝTA** [at'ɪda'r'i:ta]
CLOSED	**UŽDARÝTA** [ʊʒda'r'i:ta]
FOR WOMEN	**MÓTERŲ** ['mot'ɛru:]
FOR MEN	**VÝRŲ** ['v'i:ru:]
GENTLEMEN, GENTS (m)	**VÝRŲ** ['v'i:ru:]
WOMEN (f)	**MÓTERŲ** ['mot'ɛru:]
DISCOUNTS	**NÚOLAIDOS** ['nʊolʲʌɪdos]
SALE	**IŠPARDAVÌMAS** [ɪʃparda'v'ɪmas]
FREE	**NEMÓKAMAI** [n'ɛ'mokamʌɪ]
NEW!	**NAUJÍENA!** [nɑʊ'jiɛna!]
ATTENTION!	**DĖMESIO!** ['d'e:mes'oǁ]
NO VACANCIES	**LAISVŲ VIĖTŲ NĖRÀ** [l'ʌɪs'vu: 'v'ɛtu: n'e:'ra]
RESERVED	**REZERVÚOTA** [r'ɛz'ɛr'vʊota]
ADMINISTRATION	**ADMINISTRÃCIJA** [adm'ɪn'ɪs'tra:ts'ɪja]
STAFF ONLY	**TÌK PERSONÃLUI** ['t'ɪk p'ɛrso'nal'ʊi]

BEWARE OF THE DOG!	**ATSARGIAĬ, ŠUŐ!** [atsarˈɡʲɛɪ, ˈʃʊɑ!]
NO SMOKING!	**NERŪKÝTI!** [nʲɛruːˈkʲiːtʲɪ!]
DO NOT TOUCH!	**NELIĖSTI!** [nʲɛˈlʲɛstʲɪ!]
DANGEROUS	**PAVOJÌNGA** [pavoˈjɪnga]
DANGER	**PAVŐJUS** [paˈvoːjʊs]
HIGH VOLTAGE	**AUKŠTÀ ĮTAMPA** [ɑʊkʃˈta ˈiːtampa]
NO SWIMMING!	**NESIMÁUDYTI!** [nʲɛsʲɪˈmɑʊdʲiːtʲɪ!]
OUT OF ORDER	**NEVEĬKIA** [nʲɛˈvʲɛɪkʲæ]
FLAMMABLE	**DEGÙ** [dʲɛˈɡʊ]
FORBIDDEN	**UŽDRAUSTÀ** [ʊʒdrɑʊsˈta]
NO TRESPASSING!	**PRAĖJÌMO NĖRÀ!** [praʲeːˈjɪmɔ nʲeːˈra!]
WET PAINT	**DAŽÝTA** [daˈʒiːta]
CLOSED FOR RENOVATIONS	**UŽDARÝTA REMŐNTUI** [ʊʒdaˈrʲiːta rʲɛˈmontʊi]
WORKS AHEAD	**KĖLIO DARBAĬ** [ˈkʲælʲɔ darˈbʌɪ]
DETOUR	**APÝLANKA** [aˈpʲiːlʲanka]

Transportation. General phrases

plane	**lėktùvas** [lʲeːkˈtʊvas]
train	**traukinỹs** [trɑʊkʲɪˈnʲiːs]
bus	**autobùsas** [ɑʊtoˈbʊsas]
ferry	**keĺtas** [ˈkʲɛlʲtas]
taxi	**taksì** [takˈsʲɪ]
car	**automobìlis** [ɑʊtomoˈbʲɪlʲɪs]

schedule	**tvarkãraštis** [tvarˈkaːraʃtʲɪs]
Where can I see the schedule?	**Kuȓ galiù ràsti tvarkãraštį?** [ˈkʊr gaˈlʲʊ ˈrastʲɪ tvarˈkaːraʃtʲɪː?]
workdays (weekdays)	**dárbo dienomìs** [ˈdarbɔ dʲiɛnoˈmʲɪs]
weekends	**savàitgaliais** [saˈvʌɪtgalʲɛɪs]
holidays	**šveñtinėmis dienomìs** [ˈʃvɛntʲɪnʲeːmʲɪs dʲiɛnoˈmʲɪs]

DEPARTURE	**IŠVYKÌMAS** [ɪʃvʲiːˈkʲɪmas]
ARRIVAL	**ATVYKÌMAS** [atvʲiːˈkʲɪmas]
DELAYED	**ATIDĖTAS** [atʲɪˈdʲeːtas]
CANCELLED	**ÀTŠAUKTAS** [ˈatʃɑʊktas]

next (train, etc.)	**kìtas** [ˈkʲɪtas]
first	**pìrmas** [ˈpʲɪrmas]
last	**paskutìnis** [paskʊˈtʲɪnʲɪs]

When is the next ...?	**Kadà kìtas ...?** [kaˈda ˈkʲɪtas ...?]
When is the first ...?	**Kadà pìrmas ...?** [kaˈda ˈpʲɪrmas ...?]

When is the last ...?

Kadà paskutìnis ...?
[ka'da paskʊ'tʲɪnʲɪs ...?]

transfer (change of trains, etc.)

pérsėdimas
['pʲɛrsʲeːdʲɪmas]

to make a transfer

pérsėsti
['pʲɛrsʲeːstʲɪ]

Do I need to make a transfer?

Aȓ màn reìkia pérsėsti?
[ar 'man 'rʲɛɪkʲɛ 'pʲærsʲeːstʲɪ?]

Buying tickets

Where can I buy tickets?	**Kur galiu nusipirkti bilietą?** ['kʊr ga'lʲʊ nʊsʲɪ'pʲɪrktʲɪ 'bʲɪlʲiɛta:?]
ticket	**bilietas** ['bʲɪlʲiɛtas]
to buy a ticket	**nusipirkti bilietą** [nʊsʲɪ'pʲɪrktʲɪ 'bʲɪlʲiɛta:]
ticket price	**bilieto kaina** ['bʲɪlʲiɛto 'kʌɪna]
Where to?	**Į kur?** [i: 'kʊr?]
To what station?	**Į kurią stotį?** [i: kʊ'rʲæ: 'sto:tʲɪ?]
I need ...	**Man reikia ...** ['man 'rʲɛɪkʲɛ ...]
one ticket	**vieno bilieto** ['vʲiɛno 'bʲɪlʲiɛto]
two tickets	**dviejų bilietų** [dvʲiɛ'ju: 'bʲɪlʲiɛtu:]
three tickets	**trijų bilietų** [trʲɪ'ju: 'bʲɪlʲiɛtu:]
one-way	**į vieną pusę** [i: 'vʲiɛna: 'pʊsʲɛ:]
round-trip	**pirmyn - atgal** [pʲɪr'mʲi:n - at'galʲ]
first class	**pirmąja klasė** [pʲɪr'ma:ja klʲa'sʲɛ]
second class	**antrąja klasė** [ant'ra:ja klʲa'sʲɛ]
today	**šiandien** ['ʃændʲiɛn]
tomorrow	**rytoj** [rʲɪ'toj]
the day after tomorrow	**poryt** [po'rʲi:t]
in the morning	**rytė** [rʲɪ'tʲɛ]
in the afternoon	**po pietų** ['po: pʲiɛ'tu:]
in the evening	**vakarė** [vaka'rʲɛ]

aisle seat	**vietà priẽ praėjìmo** [vʲiɛˈta prʲɛ praʲeːˈjɪmɔ]
window seat	**vietà priẽ lángo** [vʲiɛˈta prʲɛ ˈlʲangɔ]
How much?	**Kíek?** [ˈkʲiɛk?]
Can I pay by credit card?	**Ar̃ galiù mokéti kredìto kortelė̃?** [ar gaˈlʲʊ mɔˈkʲeːtʲɪ krɛˈdʲɪtɔ kɔrteˈlʲɛ?]

Bus

bus	**autobùsas** [ɑʊtoˈbʊsas]
intercity bus	**tarpmiestìnis autobùsas** [tarpmʲiɛsˈtʲɪnʲɪs ɑʊtoˈbʊsas]
bus stop	**autobùsų stotẽlė** [ɑʊtoˈbʊsuː stoˈtʲælʲeː]
Where's the nearest bus stop?	**Kur̃ yrà arčiáusia autobùsų stotẽlė?** [ˈkʊr iːˈra arˈtʃʲæʊsʲɛ ɑʊtoˈbʊsuː stoˈtʲælʲe:?]
number (bus ~, etc.)	**nùmeris** [ˈnʊmʲɛrʲɪs]
Which bus do I take to get to ...?	**Kuriuõ autobusù galimà nuvažiúoti į̃ ...?** [kʊˈrʲʊo: ɑʊtobʊˈsʊ galʲɪˈma nʊvaˈʒʲʊotʲɪ iː ...?]
Does this bus go to ...?	**Ar̃ šìs autobùsas važiúoja į̃ ...?** [ar ʃɪːs ɑʊtoˈbʊsas vaˈʒʲʊo:jɛ iː ...?]
How frequent are the buses?	**Kàs kíek laĩko važiúoja autobùsai?** [ˈkas ˈkʲiɛk ˈlʲʌɪkɔ vaˈʒʲʊɑ:jɛ ɑʊtoˈbʊsʌɪ?]
every 15 minutes	**kàs penkiólika minùčių** [ˈkas pʲɛŋˈkʲolʲɪka mʲɪˈnʊtʃʲu:]
every half hour	**kàs pùsvalandį** [ˈkas ˈpʊsvalʲandʲɪ:]
every hour	**kàs vãlandą** [ˈkas ˈvaːlʲanda:]
several times a day	**Kelìs kartùs per̃ diẽną** [kʲɛˈlʲɪs karˈtʊs pʲɛr ˈdʲɛna:]
... times a day	**... kartùs per̃ diẽną** [... karˈtʊs pʲɛr ˈdʲɛna:]
schedule	**tvarkãraštis** [tvarˈka:raʃtʲɪs]
Where can I see the schedule?	**Kur̃ galiù ràsti tvarkãraštį?** [ˈkʊr gaˈlʲʊ ˈrastʲɪ tvarˈka:raʃtʲɪ:?]
When is the next bus?	**Kadà kìtas autobùsas?** [kaˈda ˈkʲɪtas ɑʊtoˈbʊsas?]
When is the first bus?	**Kadà pìrmas autobùsas?** [kaˈda ˈpʲɪrmas ɑʊtoˈbʊsas?]
When is the last bus?	**Kadà paskutìnis autobùsas?** [kaˈda paskʊˈtʲɪnʲɪs ɑʊtoˈbʊsas?]

stop	**stotelė** [stoˈtʲælʲeː]
next stop	**kita stotelė** [kɪˈta stoˈtʲælʲeː]
last stop (terminus)	**paskutinė maršruto stotelė** [paskuˈtʲɪnʲeː marʃˈrutɔ stoˈtʲælʲeː]
Stop here, please.	**Prašau, sustokite čia.** [praˈʃɑu, susˈtokʲɪtʲɛ tʂʲæ.]
Excuse me, this is my stop.	**Atsiprašau, tai mano stotelė.** [atsʲɪpraˈʃɑu, tʌɪ ˈmaːnɔ stoˈtʲælʲeː.]

Train

train	**traukinỹs** [trɑʊkʲɪˈrʲnʲiːs]
suburban train	**priemiestìnis traukinỹs** [prʲiɛmʲiɛsˈtʲɪnʲɪs trɑʊkʲɪˈrʲnʲiːs]
long-distance train	**tarpmiestìnis traukinỹs** [tarpmʲiɛsˈtʲɪnʲɪs trɑʊkʲɪˈrʲnʲiːs]
train station	**traukinių̃ stotìs** [trɑʊkʲɪnʲuː stoˈtʲɪs]
Excuse me, where is the exit to the platform?	**Atsiprašaũ, kur̃ yrà išėjìmas į̃ peroną?** [atsʲɪpraˈʃɑʊ, kʊr iːˈra iʃeːˈjɪmas iː peˈrona:?]
Does this train go to …?	**Ar̃ šìs traukinỹs važiúoja į̃ …?** [ar ʃɪːs trɑʊkʲɪˈrʲnʲɪːs vaˈʒʲʊoːjɛ iː …?]
next train	**kìtas traukinỹs** [ˈkʲɪtas trɑʊkʲɪˈrʲnʲiːs]
When is the next train?	**Kadà kìtas traukinỹs?** [kaˈda kʲɪtas trɑʊkʲɪˈrʲnʲiːs?]
Where can I see the schedule?	**Kur̃ galiù ràsti tvarkãraštį?** [ˈkʊr gaˈlʲʊ ˈrastʲɪ tvarˈka:raʃtʲɪ?]
From which platform?	**Ìš kuriõ peròno?** [ɪʃ kʊˈrʲoː pʲɛˈrono?]
When does the train arrive in …?	**Kadà traukinỹs atvažiuõs į̃ …?** [kaˈda trɑʊkʲɪˈrʲnʲɪːs atvaˈʒʲʊoːs iː …?]
Please help me.	**Prašaũ, padékite mán.** [praˈʃɑʊ, paˈdʲeːkʲɪte ˈman.]
I'm looking for my seat.	**Ìeškau sàvo viẽtos.** [ˈrʲɛʃkɑʊ ˈsavɔ ˈvʲɛtos.]
We're looking for our seats.	**Ìeškome sàvo viẽtų.** [ˈrʲɛʃkomʲɛ ˈsavɔ ˈvʲɛtuː.]
My seat is taken.	**Màno vietà užimtà.** [ˈmanɔ vʲiɛˈta ʊʒʲɪmˈta.]
Our seats are taken.	**Mū́sų viẽtos ùžimtos.** [ˈmuːsu: ˈvʲɛtos ˈʊʒʲɪmtos.]
I'm sorry but this is my seat.	**Atsiprašaũ, bèt taĩ màno vietà.** [atsʲɪpraˈʃɑʊ, bʲɛt tʌɪ ˈmanɔ vʲiɛˈta.]
Is this seat taken?	**Ar̃ šì vietà užimtà?** [ar ʃɪ vʲiɛˈta ʊʒʲɪmˈta?]
May I sit here?	**Ar̃ galiù čià atsisésti?** [ar gaˈlʲʊ ˈtʂʲæ atsʲɪˈsʲeːstʲɪ?]

On the train. Dialogue (No ticket)

Ticket, please.
Prašaū paródyti bìlietą.
[pra'ʃɑʊ pa'rodⁱi:tⁱɪ bⁱɪlⁱiɛta:.]

I don't have a ticket.
Àš neturiù bìlieto.
['aʃ nⁱɛtu'rⁱʊ 'bⁱɪlⁱiɛtɔ.]

I lost my ticket.
Pàmečiau sàvo bìlietą.
['pamⁱɛtʂⁱɛʊ 'savɔ 'bⁱɪlⁱiɛta:.]

I forgot my ticket at home.
Pamiršaū sàvo bìlietą namuosè.
[pamⁱɪr'ʃɑʊ 'savɔ 'bⁱɪlⁱiɛta: namʊɑ'sⁱɛ.]

You can buy a ticket from me.
Gãlite nusipìrkti bìlietą ìš manę̃s.
['ga:lⁱɪtⁱɛ nʊsⁱɪ'pⁱɪrktⁱɪ 'bⁱɪlⁱiɛta: ɪʃ ma'nⁱɛ:s.]

You will also have to pay a fine.
Taĩp pàt turėsite sumokéti baũdą.
['tʌɪp 'pat tu'rⁱe:sⁱɪte sʊmo'kⁱe:tⁱɪ 'baʊda:.]

Okay.
Geraĩ.
[gⁱɛ'rʌɪ.]

Where are you going?
Kur̃ važiúojate?
['kʊr va'ʒⁱʊo:jɛtⁱɛ?]

I'm going to …
Važiúoju į̃ …
[va'ʒⁱʊo:jʊ i: …]

How much? I don't understand.
Kíek? Àš nesuprantù.
['kⁱiɛk? aʃ nⁱɛsʊpran'tʊ.]

Write it down, please.
Ar̃ gãlite užrašýti?
[ar 'ga:lⁱɪtⁱɛ ʊʒra'ʃɪ:tⁱɪ?]

Okay. Can I pay with a credit card?
Geraĩ. Ar̃ galiù mokéti kredìto kortele?
[gⁱɛ'rʌɪ. ar ga'lⁱʊ mo'kⁱe:tⁱɪ kre'dⁱɪtɔ korte'lⁱɛ?]

Yes, you can.
Taĩp, gãlite.
['tʌɪp, 'ga:lⁱɪtⁱɛ.]

Here's your receipt.
Štaĩ jū́sų čẽkis.
['ʃtʌɪ 'ju:su: 'tʂⁱɛkⁱɪs.]

Sorry about the fine.
Atsiprašaū dė̃l baudõs.
[atsⁱɪpra'ʃɑʊ dⁱe:lⁱ bɑʊ'dɔ:s.]

That's okay. It was my fault.
Niẽko, taĩ máno kaltė̃.
['nⁱiɛkɔ, 'tʌɪ 'ma:nɔ kalⁱ'tⁱe:.]

Enjoy your trip.
Gẽros kelionė̃s.
['gⁱɛrɔ:s kⁱɛ'lⁱionⁱɛs.]

Taxi

taxi
taksì
[tak'sʲɪ]

taxi driver
taksì vairúotojas
[tak'sʲɪ vʌɪ'ruoto:jɛs]

to catch a taxi
susistabdýti taksì
[sʊsʲɪstab'dʲi:tʲɪ tak'sʲɪ]

taxi stand
taksì stotẽlė
[tak'sʲɪ sto'tʲælʲe:]

Where can I get a taxi?
Kũr galiù išsikviẽsti taksì?
['kʊr ga'lʲʊ ɪʃʲɪk'vʲɛstʲɪ tak'sʲɪ?]

to call a taxi
išsikviẽsti taksì
[ɪʃʲɪ'kvʲɛstʲɪ tak'sʲɪ]

I need a taxi.
Mán reĩkia taksì.
['man 'rʲɛɪkʲɛ tak'sʲɪ.]

Right now.
Dabãr.
[da'bar.]

What is your address (location)?
Kóks jū́sų ãdresas?
['koks 'ju:su: 'a:drʲɛsas?]

My address is ...
Màno ãdresas yrà...
['manɔ 'a:drʲɛsas i:'ra...]

Your destination?
Kũr važiúosite?
['kʊr va'ʒʲuosʲɪtʲɛ?]

Excuse me, ...
Atsiprašaũ, ...
[atsʲɪpra'ʃɑʊ, ...]

Are you available?
Ar̃ Jū̃s neùžimtas?
[ar 'ju:s 'nʲɛʊ ʒʲɪmtas?]

How much is it to get to ...?
Kíek kainúotų nuvažiúoti į̃ ...?
['kʲɪɛk kʌɪ'nuotu: nʊva'ʒʲuotʲɪ i: ...?]

Do you know where it is?
Ar̃ žìnote, kũr taĩ yrà?
[ar 'ʒʲɪnotʲɛ, kʊr tʌɪ i:'ra?]

Airport, please.
Į̃ óro úostą.
[i: 'orɔ 'uasta:.]

Stop here, please.
Sustókite čià, prašaũ.
[sʊs'tokʲɪtʲɛ tʂʲæ, pra'ʃɑʊ.]

It's not here.
Taĩ nè čià.
['tʌɪ nʲɛ 'tʂʲæ.]

This is the wrong address.
Čià nè tàs ãdresas.
['tʂʲæ nʲɛ 'tas 'a:drʲɛsas.]

Turn left.
Sùkite kairẽn.
['sʊkʲɪtʲɛ kʌɪ'rʲe:n.]

Turn right.
Sùkite dešinẽn.
['sʊkʲɪtʲɛ deʃʲɪ'nʲe:n.]

How much do I owe you?

Kíek aš skolìngas/skolìnga?
['kʲiɛk aʃ sko'lʲɪngas /sko'lʲɪnga?/]

I'd like a receipt, please.

Noréčiau čèkio.
[no'rʲe:tʂʲɛʊ 'tʂʲɛkʲɔ.]

Keep the change.

Grąžą pasilìkite.
[gra:'ʒa: pasʲɪ'lʲɪkʲɪtʲɛ.]

Would you please wait for me?

Prašaũ mãnęs palaúkti.
[pra'ʃɑʊ 'ma:nʲɛ:s pa'lʲɑʊktʲɪ.]

five minutes

penkiàs minutès
[pʲɛŋ'kʲæs mʲɪnʊ'tʲɛs]

ten minutes

dẽšimt minùčių
['dʲæʃɪmt mʲɪ'nʊtʂʲu:]

fifteen minutes

penkiólika minùčių
[pʲɛŋ'kʲolʲɪka mʲɪ'nʊtʂʲu:]

twenty minutes

dvìdešimt minùčių
['dvʲɪdʲɛʃɪmt mʲɪ'nʊtʂʲu:]

half an hour

pùsvalandį
['pʊsvalʲandʲɪ:]

Hotel

Hello.	**Sveikì.** [sv'ɛɪ'k'ɪ.]
My name is ...	**Mãno var̃das ...** ['ma:nɔ 'vardas ...]
I have a reservation.	**Àš rezervavaũ kam̃barį.** ['aʃ r'ɛz'ɛrva'vɑʊ 'kambar'ɪ:.]
I need ...	**Màn reĩkia ...** ['man 'r'ɛɪk'ɛ ...]
a single room	**kam̃bario vienám žmógui** ['kambar'ɔ v'ɪɛ'nam 'ʒmogʊi]
a double room	**kam̃bario dviems žmonéms** ['kambar'ɔ 'dv'iɛms ʒmo'n'e:ms]
How much is that?	**Kíek taĩ kainuõs?** ['k'iɛk 'tʌɪ kʌɪ'nuɑs?]
That's a bit expensive.	**Trupùtį brangù.** [trʊ'pʊti: bran'gʊ.]
Do you have anything else?	**Ar̃ tùrite kažką̃ kìto?** [ar 'tʊr'ɪt'ɛ kaʒ'ka: 'k'ɪto?]
I'll take it.	**Paim̃siu.** ['pʌɪms'ʊ.]
I'll pay in cash.	**Mokésiu grynaìs.** [mo'k'e:s'ʊ gr'i:'nʌɪs.]
I've got a problem.	**Turiù problèmą.** [tʊ'r'ʊ prob'l'ɛma:.]
My ... is broken.	**Sulū̃žo màno ...** [sʊ'l'u:ʒo 'manɔ ...]
My ... is out of order.	**Neveĩkia màno ... .** [n'ɛ'v'ɛɪk'ɛ 'manɔ ...]
TV	**televìzorius** [t'ɛl'ɛ'v'ɪzor'ʊs]
air conditioner	**óro kondicioniẽrius** ['orɔ kond'ɪts'ɪjo'n'ɛr'ʊs]
tap	**čiáupas** ['tʂ'æʊpas]
shower	**dùšas** ['dʊʃas]
sink	**praustùvė** [prɑʊs'tʊv'e:]
safe	**seĩfas** ['s'ɛɪfas]

door lock	**durų spyna** [dʊ'ru: spʲi:'na]
electrical outlet	**elektros lizdas** [ɛ'lʲɛktros 'lʲɪzdas]
hairdryer	**plaukų džiovintuvas** [plʲɑʊ'ku: dʒʲovʲɪn'tʊvas]

I don't have ...	**Aš neturiu ...** ['aʃ nʲɛtʊ'rʲʊ ...]
water	**vandens** [van'dʲɛns]
light	**šviesos** [ʃvʲiɛ'so:s]
electricity	**elektros** [ɛ'lʲɛktros]

Can you give me ...?	**Ar galite duoti ...?** [ar 'ga:lʲɪtʲɛ 'dʊotʲɪ ...?]
a towel	**rankšluostį** ['raŋkʃlʲʊɑsti:]
a blanket	**antklodę** ['antklʲodʲɛ:]
slippers	**šlepetès** [ʃlʲɛpʲɛ'tʲɛs]
a robe	**chalatą** [xa'lʲa:ta:]
shampoo	**šampūno** [ʃam'pu:nɔ]
soap	**muilo** ['mʊɪlʲɔ]

I'd like to change rooms.	**Norėčiau pakeisti kambarį.** [no'rʲe:tʃʲɛʊ pa'kʲɛɪstʲɪ 'kambarʲɪ:.]
I can't find my key.	**Nerandu savo rakto.** [nʲɛran'dʊ 'savo 'ra:ktɔ.]
Could you open my room, please?	**Ar galite atrakinti mano kambarį?** [ar 'ga:lʲɪtʲɛ atrakʲɪ:ntʲɪ 'manɔ 'kambarʲɪ:?]
Who's there?	**Kas ten?** ['kas tʲɛn?]
Come in!	**Užeikite!** [ʊ'ʒʲɛɪkʲɪtʲɛ!]
Just a minute!	**Palaukite minutę!** [pa'lʲɑʊkʲɪtʲɛ mʲɪ'nʊtʲɛ:!]
Not right now, please.	**Ne dabar, prašau.** ['nʲɛ da'bar, pra'ʃɑʊ.]

Come to my room, please.	**Prašau, užeikite į mano kambarį.** [pra'ʃɑʊ, ʊ'ʒʲɛɪkʲɪtʲɛ i: 'manɔ 'kambarʲɪ:.]
I'd like to order food service.	**Norėčiau užsisakýti maisto.** [no'rʲe:tʃʲɛʊ ʊʒsʲɪsa'kʲi:tʲɪ 'mʌɪstɔ.]
My room number is ...	**Mano kambario numeris ...** ['ma:nɔ 'kambarʲɔ 'nʊmʲɛrʲɪs ...]

I'm leaving …

Aš išvykstu …
[ˈaʃ iʃvʲiːksˈtʊ …]

We're leaving …

Mes išvỹkstame …
[ˈmʲæs iʃˈvʲiːkstamʲɛ …]

right now

dabar̃
[daˈbar]

this afternoon

põ pietų̃
[ˈpoː pʲiɛˈtuː]

tonight

šią̃nakt
[ˈʃʲæːnakt]

tomorrow

rytój
[rʲiːˈtoj]

tomorrow morning

rýt rytè
[ˈrʲiːt rʲiːˈtʲɛ]

tomorrow evening

rýt vakarè
[ˈrʲiːt vakaˈrʲɛ]

the day after tomorrow

porýt
[poˈrʲiːt]

I'd like to pay.

Norḗčiau sumokḗti.
[noˈrʲeːtʂʲɛʊ sʊmoˈkʲeːtʲɪ.]

Everything was wonderful.

Vìskas bùvo nuostabù.
[ˈvʲɪskas ˈbʊvɔ nʊɑstaˈbʊ.]

Where can I get a taxi?

Kur̃ galiù išsikviẽsti taksì?
[ˈkʊr gaˈlʲʊ ɪʃʲɪkˈvʲɛstʲɪ takˈsʲɪ?]

Would you call a taxi for me, please?

Ar̃ galḗtumėte mán iškviẽsti taksì?
[ar gaˈlʲeːtʊmʲeːte ˈman iʃkˈvʲɛstʲɪ takˈsʲɪ?]

Restaurant

Can I look at the menu, please?
Ar galiù gáuti meniù?
[ar gaˈlʲʊ ˈɡɑʊtʲɪ mʲɛˈnʲʊ?]

Table for one.
Stãlą vienám.
['staːlʲa: vʲiɛˈnam.]

There are two (three, four) of us.
Mū̃sų dù (trỹs, keturì).
['muːsu: 'dʊ (ˈtryiːs, ketʊˈrʲɪ).]

Smoking
Rū̃kantiems
['ruːkantʲiɛms]

No smoking
Nerū̃kantiems
[nʲɛˈruːkantʲiɛms]

Excuse me! (addressing a waiter)
Atsiprašaũ!
[atsʲɪpraˈʃɑʊ!]

menu
meniù
[mʲɛˈnʲʊ]

wine list
vỹno meniù
['vʲiːnɔ mʲɛˈnʲʊ]

The menu, please.
Meniù, prašaũ.
[mʲɛˈnʲʊ, praˈʃɑʊ.]

Are you ready to order?
Ar jaũ norésite užsisakýti?
[ar jɛʊ noˈrʲeːsʲɪte ʊʒsʲɪsaˈkʲiːtʲɪ?]

What will you have?
Ką užsisakýsite?
[ka: ʊʒsʲɪsaˈkʲiːsʲɪtʲɛ?]

I'll have ...
Àš paim̃siu ...
['aʃ 'pʌɪmsʲʊ ...]

I'm a vegetarian.
Àš vegetãras /vegetãrė/.
['aʃ vegeˈtaːras /vegeˈtaːrʲe:/.]

meat
mėsõs
[mʲeːˈsoːs]

fish
žuviẽs
[ʒʊˈvʲɛs]

vegetables
daržóvės
[darˈʒovʲeːs]

Do you have vegetarian dishes?
Ar tùrite vegetãriškų patiekalų̃?
[ar ˈtʊrʲɪtʲɛ vʲɛɡʲɛˈtaːrʲɪʃku: patʲiɛkaˈlʲuː?]

I don't eat pork.
Àš neválgau kiaulíenos.
['aʃ nʲɛˈvalʲɡɑʊ kʲɛʊˈlʲiɛnos.]

He /she/ doesn't eat meat.
Jìs /jì/ neválgo mėsõs.
[jɪs /jɪ/ nɛˈvalʲɡɔ mʲeːˈsoːs.]

I am allergic to ...
Àš alèrgiškas /alèrgiška/ ...
['aʃ aˈlʲɛrɡʲɪʃkas /aˈlʲɛrɡʲɪʃka/ ...]

Would you please bring me ...	**Prašaū atnešti mán ...** [pra'ʃɑu at'nʲɛʃtʲɪ 'man ...]
salt | pepper | sugar	**druskos | pipìrų | cùkraus** ['druskos | pʲɪ'pʲɪru: | 'tsukrɑus]
coffee | tea | dessert	**kavõs | arbãtos | desèrtą** [ka'vo:s | ar'ba:tos | dʲɛ'sʲɛrta:]
water | sparkling | plain	**vandeñs | gazúoto | negazúoto** [van'dʲɛns | ga'zuoto | nʲɛga'zuoto]
a spoon | fork | knife	**šáukštą | šakùtę | peĩlį** ['ʃɑukʃta: | ʃa'kutʲɛ: | 'pʲɛɪlʲɪ:]
a plate | napkin	**lėkštę | servetėlę** [lʲe:kʃtʲɛ: | serve'tʲe:lʲɛ:]

Enjoy your meal!	**Skanaũs!** [ska'nɑus!]
One more, please.	**Prašaū dár víeną.** [pra'ʃɑu 'dar 'vʲiɛna:.]
It was very delicious.	**Bùvo lãbai skanù.** ['buvo 'lʲa:bʌɪ ska'nu.]

---

check | change | tip	**sąskaita | grąžà | arbãtpinigiai** ['sa:skʌɪta | gra:'ʒa | ar'ba:tpʲɪnʲɪgʲɛɪ]
Check, please. (Could I have the check, please?)	**Sąskaitą, prašaū.** ['sa:skʌɪta:, pra'ʃɑu.]
Can I pay by credit card?	**Aȓ galiù mokéti kredìto kortelè?** [ar ga'lʲu mo'kʲe:tʲɪ kre'dʲɪto korte'lʲɛ?]
I'm sorry, there's a mistake here.	**Atsiprašaū, bèt jū̃s suklýdote.** [atsʲɪpra'ʃɑu, bʲɛt 'ju:s suk'lʲi:dotʲɛ.]

Shopping

Can I help you?	**Kuõ galiù padéti?** ['kʊɑ ga'lʲʊ pa'dʲeːtʲɪ?]
Do you have ...?	**Ar̃ turite ...?** [ar 'tʊrʲɪtʲɛ ...?]
I'm looking for ...	**Íeškau ...** ['ɪʲɛʃkɑʊ ...]
I need ...	**Mán reĩkia ...** ['man 'rʲɛɪkʲɛ ...]

I'm just looking.	**Àš tìk apžiūrinéju.** ['aʃ tʲɪk apʒʲʊːrʲɪ'nʲeːjʊ.]
We're just looking.	**Mẽs tìk apžiūrinéjame.** ['mʲæs 'tʲɪk apʒʲʊːrʲɪ'nʲeːjame.]
I'll come back later.	**Sugrį̃šiu véliaũ.** [sʊg'rʲɪːʃʊ vʲeː'lʲɛʊ.]
We'll come back later.	**Sugrį̃šime véliaũ.** [sʊg'rʲɪːʃɪme vʲeː'lʲɛʊ.]
discounts | sale	**núolaidos | išpardavìmas** ['nʊolʲʌɪdos | ɪʃparda'vʲɪmas]

Would you please show me ...	**Paródykite mán, prašaũ, ...** [pa'rodʲɪːkʲɪtʲɛ 'man, pra'ʃɑʊ, ...]
Would you please give me ...	**Dúokite mán, prašaũ, ...** ['dʊokʲɪtʲɛ 'man, pra'ʃɑʊ, ...]
Can I try it on?	**Ar̃ galiù pasimatúoti?** [ar ga'lʲʊ pasʲɪma'tʊotʲɪ?]
Excuse me, where's the fitting room?	**Atsiprašaũ, kur̃ yrà matãvimosi kabìnos?** [atsʲɪpra'ʃɑʊ, kʊr iː'ra ma'taːvʲɪmosʲɪ ka'bʲɪnos?]
Which color would you like?	**Kokiõs spalvõs norétuméte?** [kɔ'kʲoːs spalʲʲʲvoːs no'rʲeːtʊmʲeːte?]
size | length	**dỹdis | ìlgis** ['dʲiːdʲɪs | 'ɪlʲgʲɪs]
How does it fit?	**Ar̃ tiñka?** [ar 'tʲɪŋka?]

How much is it?	**Kíek taĩ kainúoja?** ['kʲiɛk 'tʌɪ kʌɪ'nʊoːjɛ?]
That's too expensive.	**Per̃ brangù.** ['pʲɛr bran'gʊ.]
I'll take it.	**Paim̃siu.** ['pʌɪmsʲʊ.]

Excuse me, where do I pay?

Atsiprašaŭ, kur̃ galiù sumokéti?
[atsʲɪpraˈʃɑʊ, kʊr gaˈlʲʊ sʊmoˈkʲeːtʲɪ?]

Will you pay in cash or credit card?

Mokésite grynaĩs ar̃ kredìto kortelė?
[moˈkʲeːsʲɪte grʲiːˈnʌɪs ar krʲɛˈdʲɪtɔ korteˈlʲɛ?]

In cash | with credit card

grynaĩs | kredìto kortelė
[grʲiːˈnʌɪs | krʲɛˈdʲɪtɔ kortʲɛˈlʲɛ]

Do you want the receipt?

Ar̃ reĩkia čẽkio?
[ar ˈrʲɛɪkʲɛ ˈtʂʲɛkʲo?]

Yes, please.

Taĩp.
[ˈtʌɪp.]

No, it's OK.

Nè, nereĩkia.
[ˈnʲɛ, nʲɛˈrʲɛɪkʲæ.]

Thank you. Have a nice day!

Ãčiū. Vìso gẽro.
[ˈaːtʂʲuː. ˈvʲɪsɔ ˈgʲærɔ.]

In town

Excuse me, please.	**Atsiprašau, ...** [atsʲɪpraˈʃɒʋ.]
I'm looking for ...	**Ieškau ...** [ˈrʲɛʃkɒʋ ...]

the subway	**metro** [mʲɛˈtro]
my hotel	**savo viešbučio** [ˈsavɔ ˈvʲɛʃbʊtʃʲɔ]
the movie theater	**kino teatro** [ˈkʲɪnɔ tʲɛˈaːtrɔ]
a taxi stand	**taksi stotelę** [takˈsʲɪ stoˈtʲælʲɛː]

an ATM	**bankomato** [baŋkoˈmaːtɔ]
a foreign exchange office	**valiutos keitýklos** [vaˈlʲʊtos kʲɛɪˈtʲiːklos]
an internet café	**interneto kavinės** [ɪntɛrˈnʲɛtɔ kavʲɪˈnʲeːs]
... street	**... gatvės** [... gaːtˈvʲeːs]
this place	**šios vietos** [ˈʃʲoːs ˈvʲɛtos]

Do you know where ... is?	**Ar žinote, kur yra ...?** [ar ˈʒʲɪnotʲɛ, kʊr iːˈra ...?]
Which street is this?	**Kokia čia gatvė?** [kɔˈkʲæ tʃʲæ ˈgaːtvʲeː?]

Show me where we are right now.	**Paródykite, kur dabar esame.** [paˈrodʲiːkʲɪtʲɛ, kʊr daˈbar ˈɛsamʲɛ.]
Can I get there on foot?	**Ar galiu nueiti ten pėsčiomis?** [ar gaˈlʲʊ ˈnʊʲɛɪtʲɪ ten pʲeːstʃʲoˈmʲɪs?]
Do you have a map of the city?	**Ar turite miesto žemėlapį?** [ar ˈtʊrʲɪtʲe ˈmʲɪːɛstɔ ʒeˈmʲeːˈlʲapʲɪ:?]

How much is a ticket to get in?	**Kiek kainúoja įėjimo bilietas?** [ˈkʲiɛk kʌɪˈnʊɑːjɛ iːˈeːjɪmɔ ˈbʲɪlʲietas?]
Can I take pictures here?	**Ar čia galima fotografúoti?** [ar ˈtʃʲæ galʲɪˈma fotograˈfʊotʲɪ?]
Are you open?	**Ar jūs veikiate?** [ar ˈjuːs ˈvʲɛɪkʲætʲɛ?]

When do you open?

Kadà atsidãrote?
[ka'da ats^jɪ'da:rotⁱɛ?]

When do you close?

Kadà užsidãrote?
[ka'da ʊʒs^jɪ'da:rotⁱɛ?]

Money

money	**pinigai** [pʲɪnʲɪ'gʌɪ]
cash	**grynieji** [grʲiː'nʲiɛjɪ]
paper money	**banknotai** [baŋk'notʌɪ]
loose change	**monètos** [mo'nʲɛtos]
check | change | tip	**sąskaita | grąžà | arbàtpinigiai** ['saːskʌɪta | graː'ʒa | arʲ'baːtpʲɪnʲɪgʲɛɪ]
credit card	**kredìto kortèlė** [krʲɛ'dʲɪtɔ kor'tʲælʲeː]
wallet	**piniginė** [pʲɪnʲɪ'gʲɪnʲe:]
to buy	**pirkti** ['pʲɪrktʲɪ]
to pay	**mokéti** [mo'kʲeːtʲɪ]
fine	**baudà** [bɑʊ'da]
free	**nemókamai** [nʲɛ'mokamʌɪ]
Where can I buy ...?	**Kur̃ galiù nusipirkti ...?** ['kʊr ga'lʲʊ nʊsʲɪ'pʲɪrktʲɪ ...?]
Is the bank open now?	**Ar̃ bánkas jaũ dìrba?** [ar 'baŋkas 'jɛʊ 'dʲɪrba?]
When does it open?	**Kadà atsidãro?** [ka'da atsʲɪ'da:ro?]
When does it close?	**Kadà užsidãro?** [ka'da ʊʒsʲɪ'da:ro?]
How much?	**Kíek?** ['kʲiɛk?]
How much is this?	**Kíek taĩ kainúoja?** ['kʲiɛk 'tʌɪ kʌɪ'nʊo:jɛ?]
That's too expensive.	**Per̃ brangù.** ['pʲɛr bran'gʊ.]
Excuse me, where do I pay?	**Atsiprašaũ, kur̃ galiù sumokéti?** [atsʲɪpra'ʃɑʊ, kʊr ga'lʲʊ sʊmo'kʲeːtʲɪ?]
Check, please.	**Čekį, prašaũ.** ['tʃʲɛkʲɪː, pra'ʃɑʊ.]

Can I pay by credit card?

Ar̃ galiù mokéti kredìto kortelè?
[ar ga'lʲʊ mo'kʲeːtʲɪ kre'dʲɪtɔ korte'lʲɛ?]

Is there an ATM here?

Ar̃ čià yrà bankomãtas?
[' tsʲæ iː'ra baŋko'maːtas?]

I'm looking for an ATM.

Íeškau bankomãto.
['ɪʲɛʃkɑʊ baŋko'maːtɔ.]

I'm looking for a foreign exchange office.

Íeškau valiùtos keitỹklos.
['ɪʲɛʃkɑʊ va'lʲʊtos kʲɛr'tʲiːklos.]

I'd like to change ...

Nóriu pasikeĩsti ...
['norʲʊ pasʲɪ'kʲɛɪstʲɪ ...]

What is the exchange rate?

Kóks valiùtos kùrsas?
['koks va'lʲʊtos 'kʊrsas?]

Do you need my passport?

Ar̃ reĩkia màno pãso?
[ar 'rʲɛɪkʲɛ 'manɔ 'paːsɔ?]

Time

What time is it?	**Kíek dabar̃ valandų̃?** ['kʲiɛk da'bar valʲan'du:?]
When?	**Kadà?** [ka'da?]
At what time?	**Kadà?** [ka'da?]
now | later | after ...	**dabar̃ | vėliaũ | põ ...** [da'bar | vʲe:'lʲɛʊ | 'po: ...]

one o'clock	**pìrmą vãlandą** ['pʲɪrma: 'va:lʲanda:]
one fifteen	**põ pirmõs penkiólika** ['po: pʲɪr'mo:s pʲɛŋ'kʲolʲɪka]
one thirty	**pùsė dviejų̃** ['pʊsʲe: dvʲɪɛ'ju:]
one forty-five	**bè penkiólikos dvì** ['bʲɛ pʲɛŋ'kʲolʲɪkos dvʲɪ]

one | two | three	**pirmà | antrà | trečià** [pʲɪr'ma | an'tra | trʲɛ'tsʲæ]
four | five | six	**ketvirtà | penktà | šeštà** [kʲɛtvʲɪr'ta | pʲɛŋk'ta | ʃɛʃ'ta]
seven | eight | nine	**septintà | aštuntà | devintà** [sʲɛptʲɪn'ta | aʃtʊn'ta | dʲɛvʲɪn'ta]
ten | eleven | twelve	**dešimtà | vienúolikta | dvýlikta** [dʲɛʃɪm'ta | vʲɪɛ'nʊolʲɪkta | 'dvʲi:lʲɪkta]

in ...	**ùž ...** ['ʊʒ ...]
five minutes	**penkių̃ minùčių** [pʲɛŋ'kʲu: mʲɪ'nʊtsʲu:]
ten minutes	**dẽšimt minùčių** ['dʲæʃɪmt mʲɪ'nʊtsʲu:]
fifteen minutes	**penkiólikos minùčių** [pʲɛŋ'kʲolʲɪkos mʲɪ'nʊtsʲu:]
twenty minutes	**dvìdešimt minùčių** ['dvʲɪdʲɛʃɪmt mʲɪ'nʊtsʲu:]

half an hour	**pùsvalandžio** ['pʊsvalʲandʒʲɔ]
an hour	**valandõs** [valʲan'do:s]

in the morning	rytè [rʲiː'tʲɛ]
early in the morning	ankstì rytè [aŋk'stʲɪ rʲiː'tʲɛ]
this morning	šį̃ryt ['ʃɪːrʲɪːt]
tomorrow morning	rýt rytè ['rʲiːt rʲiː'tʲɛ]

in the middle of the day	per̃ pietùs ['pʲɛr pʲiɛ'tʊs]
in the afternoon	põ pietų̃ ['poː pʲiɛ'tuː]
in the evening	vakarè [vaka'rʲɛ]
tonight	šią̃nakt ['ʃæːnakt]

at night	nãktį ['naːktiː]
yesterday	vãkar ['vaːkar]
today	šiañdien ['ʃændʲiɛn]
tomorrow	rytój [rʲiː'toj]
the day after tomorrow	porýt [po'rʲiːt]

What day is it today?	Kokià šiañdien dienà? [ko'kʲæ 'ʃændʲiɛn dʲiɛ'na?]
It's ...	Šiañdien yrà ... ['ʃændʲiɛn iː'ra ...]
Monday	pirmãdienis [pʲɪr'maːdʲiɛnʲɪs]
Tuesday	antrãdienis [an'traːdʲiɛnʲɪs]
Wednesday	trečiãdienis [trʲɛ'tʃʲædʲiɛnʲɪs]

Thursday	ketvirtãdienis [kʲɛtvʲɪr'taːdʲiɛnʲɪs]
Friday	penktãdienis [pʲɛŋk'taːdʲiɛnʲɪs]
Saturday	šeštãdienis [ʃɛʃ'taːdʲiɛnʲɪs]
Sunday	sekmãdienis [sʲɛk'maːdʲiɛnʲɪs]

Greetings. Introductions

Hello.
Sveikì.
[sv⸍ɛɪ'k⸍ɪ.]

Pleased to meet you.
Malonù susipažìnti.
[mal⸍o'nʊ sʊs⸍ɪpa'ʒ⸍ɪnt⸍ɪ.]

Me too.
Mán ir̃gi.
['man 'irg⸍ɪ.]

I'd like you to meet …
Nóriu, kàd susipažìntum sù …
['nor⸍ʊ, 'kad sʊs⸍ɪpa'ʒ⸍ɪntʊm 'sʊ …]

Nice to meet you.
Malonù susipažìnti.
[mal⸍o'nʊ sʊs⸍ɪpa'ʒ⸍ɪnt⸍ɪ.]

How are you?
Kaĩp laĩkotės?
['kʌɪp 'l⸍ʌɪkot⸍e:s?]

My name is …
Mãno var̃das …
['ma:nɔ vardas …]

His name is …
Jõ var̃das …
[jɔ: 'vardas …]

Her name is …
Jì vardù …
['jɪ var'dʊ …]

What's your name?
Kuõ jū̃s vardù?
['kʊɑ 'ju:s var'dʊ?]

What's his name?
Kuõ jìs vardù?
['kʊɑ jɪs var'dʊ?]

What's her name?
Kuõ jì vardù?
['kʊɑ jɪ var'dʊ?]

What's your last name?
Kokià jū́sų pavardė̃?
[ko'k⸍æ 'ju:su: pavar'd⸍e:?]

You can call me …
Gãli manè vadìnti …
['ga:l⸍ɪ ma'n⸍ɛ va'd⸍ɪnt⸍ɪ …]

Where are you from?
Ìš kur̃ jū̃s ẽsate?
[ɪʃ 'kʊr 'ju:s 'ɛsat⸍ɛ?]

I'm from …
Àš ìš …
['aʃ ɪʃ …]

What do you do for a living?
Kuõ užsìimate?
['kʊɑ ʊʒ's⸍ɪɪmat⸍ɛ?]

Who is this?
Kàs tàs žmogùs?
['kas 'tas ʒmo'gʊs?]

Who is he?
Kàs jìs?
['kas 'jɪs?]

Who is she?
Kàs jì?
['kas jɪ?]

Who are they?	**Kàs jiẽ?** ['kas jɪɛ?]
This is ...	**Taĩ ...** ['tʌɪ ...]
my friend (masc.)	**mãno draũgas** ['maːnɔ 'drɑuɡas]
my friend (fem.)	**mãno draugẽ** ['maːnɔ drɑu'ɡʲeː]
my husband	**mãno výras** ['maːnɔ 'vʲiːras]
my wife	**mãno žmonà** ['maːnɔ ʒmo'na]
my father	**mãno tévas** ['manɔ 'tʲeːvas]
my mother	**mãno mamà** ['maːnɔ ma'ma]
my brother	**mãno brólis** ['maːnɔ 'brolʲɪs]
my sister	**mãno sesuõ** ['maːnɔ sʲɛ'suɑ]
my son	**mãno sūnùs** ['maːnɔ suː'nʊs]
my daughter	**mãno dukrà** ['maːnɔ dʊk'ra]
This is our son.	**Taĩ mū́sų sūnùs.** ['tʌɪ 'muːsuː suː'nʊs.]
This is our daughter.	**Taĩ mū́sų dukrà.** ['tʌɪ 'muːsuː dʊk'ra.]
These are my children.	**Taĩ mãno vaikaĩ.** ['tʌɪ 'maːnɔ vʌɪ'kʌɪ.]
These are our children.	**Taĩ mū́sų vaikaĩ.** ['tʌɪ 'muːsuː vʌɪ'kʌɪ.]

Farewells

Good bye!
Vìso gẽro!
['vʲɪsɔ 'gʲæro!]

Bye! (inform.)
Ikì!
[ɪ'kʲɪ!]

See you tomorrow.
Pasimatýsim rýt.
[pasʲɪma'tʲiːsʲɪm 'rʲiːt.]

See you soon.
Greĩtai pasimatýsime.
['grʲɛɪtʌɪ pasʲɪma'tʲiːsʲɪmʲɛ.]

See you at seven.
Pasimatýsime septiñtą.
[pasʲɪma'tʲiːsʲɪmʲɛ sʲɛp'tʲɪnta:.]

Have fun!
Pasilìnksminkite!
[pasʲɪ'lʲɪŋksmʲɪŋkʲɪtʲɛ!]

Talk to you later.
Pašnekẽsim vẽliaũ.
[paʃnʲɛ'kʲeːsʲɪm vʲeːʲlʲɛʊ.]

Have a nice weekend.
Gẽro savaĩtgalio.
['gʲæro sa'vʌɪtgalʲɔ.]

Good night.
Labãnakt.
[lʲa'baːnakt.]

It's time for me to go.
Màn jaũ laĩkas eĩti.
['man 'jɛʊ 'lʲʌɪkas 'ɛɪtʲɪ.]

I have to go.
Màn reĩkia eĩti.
['man 'rʲɛɪkʲɛ 'ɛɪtʲɪ.]

I will be right back.
Tuõj grĩšiu.
['tʊɑj 'grʲɪːʃʊ.]

It's late.
Jaũ vẽlù.
['jɛʊ vʲeːʲlʲʊ.]

I have to get up early.
Màn reĩkia ankstì kéltis.
['man 'rʲɛɪkʲɛ aŋk'stʲɪ 'kʲelʲtʲɪs.]

I'm leaving tomorrow.
Àš išvykstù rýt.
['aʃ iʃvʲiːks'tʊ 'rʲiːt.]

We're leaving tomorrow.
Mẽs išvýkstame rýt.
['mʲæs iʃ'vʲiːkstamʲɛ 'rʲiːt.]

Have a nice trip!
Gẽros keliõnės!
[gʲæros kʲɛ'lʲoːnʲeːs!]

It was nice meeting you.
Bùvo malonù susipažìnti.
['bʊvɔ malʲo'nʊ sʊsʲɪpa'ʒʲɪntʲɪ.]

It was nice talking to you.
Bùvo malonù pasišnekéti.
['bʊvɔ malʲo'nʊ pasʲɪʃnʲɛ'kʲɛːtʲɪ.]

Thanks for everything.
Ãčiū ùž vìską.
['aːtʃʲuː 'ʊʒ 'vʲɪska:.]

I had a very good time.

Puikiai praléidau laiką.
[puɪkʲɛɪ praˈlʲɛɪdɑu ˈlʌɪkaː.]

We had a very good time.

Mės puikiai praléidome laiką.
[ˈmʲæs ˈpuɪkʲɛɪ praˈlʲɛɪdomʲɛ ˈlʌɪkaː.]

It was really great.

Bùvo tikraĩ smagù.
[ˈbuvɔ tʲɪkˈrʌɪ smaˈgu.]

I'm going to miss you.

Pasiĩlgsiu tavę̃s.
[pasʲɪˈlʲgsʲu taˈvʲɛːs.]

We're going to miss you.

Pasiĩlgsime jũsų.
[pasʲɪˈlʲgsʲɪmʲɛ ˈjuːsuː.]

Good luck!

Sėkmė̃s!
[sʲeːkˈmʲeːs!]

Say hi to ...

Pérduokite linkéjimus ...
[ˈpʲɛrduakʲɪtʲɛ lʲɪŋˈkʲɛjɪmus ...]

Foreign language

I don't understand.	**Nesuprantu.** [nʲɛsʊpran'tʊ.]
Write it down, please.	**Užrašykite, prašau.** [ʊʒra'ʃiːkʲɪtʲɛ, pra'ʃɑʊ.]
Do you speak ...?	**Ar kalbate ...?** [ar 'kalʲbatʲɛ ...?]

I speak a little bit of ...	**Truputį kalbu ...** [trʊ'pʊtiː kalʲˈbʊ ...]
English	**angliškai** ['anglʲɪʃkʌɪ]
Turkish	**turkiškai** ['tʊrkʲɪʃkʌɪ]
Arabic	**arabiškai** [a'ra:bʲɪʃkʌɪ]
French	**prancūziškai** [pran'tsu:zʲɪʃkʌɪ]

German	**vokiškai** ['vokʲɪʃkʌɪ]
Italian	**itališkai** [ɪ'ta:lʲɪʃkʌɪ]
Spanish	**ispaniškai** [ɪs'pa:nʲɪʃkʌɪ]
Portuguese	**portugališkai** [portʊ'ga:lʲɪʃkʌɪ]
Chinese	**kiniškai** ['kʲɪnʲɪʃkʌɪ]
Japanese	**japoniškai** [ja'ponʲɪʃkʌɪ]

Can you repeat that, please.	**Ar galite pakartoti?** [ar 'ga:lʲɪtʲɛ pakar'totʲɪ?]
I understand.	**Suprantu.** [sʊpran'tʊ.]
I don't understand.	**Nesuprantu.** [nʲɛsʊpran'tʊ.]
Please speak more slowly.	**Ar galite kalbėti lėčiau?** [ar 'ga:lʲɪte kalʲˈbʲe:tʲɪ lʲe:'tʂʲɛʊ?]

Is that correct? (Am I saying it right?)	**Ar teisingai?** [ar tʲɛɪ'sʲɪngʌɪ?]
What is this? (What does this mean?)	**Ką tai reiškia?** [ka: 'tʌɪ 'rʲɛɪʃkʲæ?]

Apologies

Excuse me, please.
Atleiskite.
[at'lɛɪskʲɪtʲɛ.]

I'm sorry.
Atsiprašaũ.
[atsʲɪpraˈʃɑʊ.]

I'm really sorry.
Mán labaĩ gaĩla.
['man lʲaˈbʌɪ ˈɡʌɪlʲa.]

Sorry, it's my fault.
Atsiprašaũ, taĩ aš káltas /kaltà/.
[atsʲɪpraˈʃɑʊ, 'tʌɪ aʃ 'kalʲtas /kal'ta/.]

My mistake.
Taĩ mãno klaidà.
['tʌɪ 'maːnɔ klʲʌɪ'da.]

May I ...?
Ar̃ galiù ...?
[ar ɡaˈlʲʊ ...?]

Do you mind if I ...?
Ar̃ jū̃s niẽko priẽš, jéi ...?
[ar 'juːs 'nʲɛkɔ 'prʲɛʃ, jɛɪ ...?]

It's OK.
Niẽko tókio.
['nʲɛkɔ 'tokʲɔ.]

It's all right.
Vìskas geraĩ.
['vʲɪskas ɡʲɛ'rʌɪ.]

Don't worry about it.
Nesijáudinkite dėl tõ.
[nʲɛsʲɪ'jɑʊdʲɪŋkʲɪte 'dʲeːlʲ 'toː.]

Agreement

Yes.	**Taĩp.** [ˈtʌɪp.]
Yes, sure.	**Žìnoma.** [ˈʒɪnoma.]
OK (Good!)	**Geraĩ.** [gʲɛˈrʌɪ.]
Very well.	**Puikù.** [puɪˈkʊ.]
Certainly!	**Būtinaĩ!** [buːtʲɪˈnʌɪ!]
I agree.	**Sutinkù.** [sʊtʲɪŋˈkʊ.]
That's correct.	**Tikraĩ.** [tʲɪkˈrʌɪ.]
That's right.	**Teisìngai.** [tʲɛɪˈsʲɪŋgʌɪ.]
You're right.	**Jũs teisùs /teisì/.** [ˈjuːs tʲɛɪˈsʊs /tʲɛɪˈsʲɪ/.]
I don't mind.	**Mán tiñka.** [ˈman ˈtʲɪŋka.]
Absolutely right.	**Tikraĩ taĩp.** [tʲɪkˈrʌɪ ˈtʌɪp.]
It's possible.	**Įmãnoma.** [iːˈmaːnoma.]
That's a good idea.	**Gerà mintìs.** [gʲɛˈra mʲɪnˈtʲɪs.]
I can't say no.	**Negaliù atsisakýti.** [nʲɛgaˈlʲʊ atsʲɪsaˈkʲiːtʲɪ.]
I'd be happy to.	**Mielaĩ.** [mʲiɛˈlʲʌɪ.]
With pleasure.	**Sù míelu nóru.** [ˈsʊ ˈmʲiɛlʲʊ ˈnorʊ.]

Refusal. Expressing doubt

No.
Nè.
['nʲɛ.]

Certainly not.
Tikraì nè.
[tʲɪk'rʌɪ nʲɛ.]

I don't agree.
Àš nesutinkù.
['aʃ nʲɛsʊtʲɪŋ'kʊ.]

I don't think so.
Nemanaũ.
[nʲɛma'nɑʊ.]

It's not true.
Taì netiesà.
['tʌɪ nʲɛtʲiɛ'sa.]

You are wrong.
Jū̃s klýstate.
['ju:s 'klʲi:statʲɛ.]

I think you are wrong.
Manaũ, jū̃s klýstate.
[ma'nɑʊ, 'ju:s 'klʲi:statʲɛ.]

I'm not sure.
Nesù tìkras /tikrà/.
[nʲɛ'sʊ 'tʲɪkras /tʲɪk'ra/.]

It's impossible.
Neįmãnoma.
[nʲɛɪ'ma:noma.]

Nothing of the kind (sort)!
Niẽko panašaũs!
['nʲɛkɔ pana'ʃɑʊs!]

The exact opposite.
Vìsiškai príešingai.
['vʲɪsʲɪʃkʌɪ 'prʲiɛʃʲɪngʌɪ.]

I'm against it.
Àš prieštaráuju.
['aʃ prʲiɛʃta'rɑʊjʊ.]

I don't care.
Mán nerū̃pi.
['man nʲɛ'ru:pʲɪ.]

I have no idea.
Neįsivaizdúoju.
[nʲɛɪsʲɪvʌɪz'dʊo:jʊ.]

I doubt it.
Abejóju.
[abʲɛ'jɔjʊ.]

Sorry, I can't.
Atsiprašaũ, bèt negaliù.
[atsʲɪpra'ʃɑʊ, bʲɛt nʲɛga'lʲʊ.]

Sorry, I don't want to.
Atsiprašaũ, bèt nenóriu.
[atsʲɪpra'ʃɑʊ, bʲɛt nʲɛ'norʲʊ.]

Thank you, but I don't need this.
Ãčiū, bèt mán nereĩkia.
['a:tʃʲu:, bʲɛt 'man nʲɛ'rʲɛɪkʲæ.]

It's getting late.
Jaũ vėlù.
['jɛʊ vʲe:'lʲʊ.]

I have to get up early.

Mán reĩkia ankstì kéltis.
['man 'rʲɛɪkʲɛ aŋk'stʲɪ 'kʲɛlʲtʲɪs.]

I don't feel well.

Nesijaučiù geraĩ.
[nʲɛsʲɪʲjɛʊ'tşʲʊ gʲɛ'rʌɪ.]

Expressing gratitude

Thank you.	**Ačiū.** ['a:tʂʲu:.]
Thank you very much.	**Labai ačiū.** [lʲa'bʌɪ 'a:tʂʲu:.]
I really appreciate it.	**Aš labai dėkingas /dėkinga/.** ['aʃ lʲa'bʌɪ dʲe:'kʲɪngas /dʲe:'kʲɪnga/.]
I'm really grateful to you.	**Labai jums dėkoju.** [lʲa'bʌɪ 'jʊms dʲe:'ko:jʊ.]
We are really grateful to you.	**Mės jums labai dėkingi.** ['mʲæs 'jʊms lʲa'bʌɪ dʲe:'kʲɪngʲɪ.]

Thank you for your time.	**Ačiū už jūsų laiką.** ['a:tʂʲu: 'ʊʒ 'juːsu: 'lʲʌɪka:.]
Thanks for everything.	**Ačiū už viską.** ['a:tʂʲu: 'ʊʒ 'vʲɪska:.]
Thank you for …	**Ačiū už …** ['a:tʂʲu: 'ʊʒ …]
your help	**pagalbą** [pa'galʲba:]
a nice time	**smagiai praleistą laiką** [sma'gʲɛɪ pra'lʲɛɪsta: 'lʌɪka:]

a wonderful meal	**nuostabų patiekalą** [nʊɑ'sta:bu: 'pa:tʲɛkalʲa:]
a pleasant evening	**malonų vakarą** [ma'lʲo:nu: 'va:kara:]
a wonderful day	**nuostabią dieną** [nʊɑ'sta:bʲæ: 'dʲɛna:]
an amazing journey	**nuostabią kelionę** [nʊɑ'sta:bʲæ: kʲɛ'lʲo:nʲɛ:]

Don't mention it.	**Nėra už ką.** [nʲe:'ra 'ʊʒ ka:.]
You are welcome.	**Nedėkokite.** [nʲɛdʲe:'kokʲɪte.]
Any time.	**Bet kada.** ['bʲɛt ka'da.]
My pleasure.	**Buvo malonu padėti.** ['bʊvɔ malʲo'nʊ pa'dʲe:tʲɪ.]
Forget it.	**Ką jūs, viskas gerai.** [ka: 'juːs, 'vʲɪskas gʲɛ'rʌɪ.]
Don't worry about it.	**Nesijáudinkite dėl tõ.** [nʲɛsʲɪ'jɑʊdʲɪnkʲɪte 'dʲe:lʲ 'to:.]

Congratulations. Best wishes

Congratulations!
Sveikinu!
['sv^jɛɪk^jɪnʊ!]

Happy birthday!
Sù gimìmo dienà!
['sʊ g^jɪ'm^jɪmɔ d^jiɛ'na!]

Merry Christmas!
Linksmų Kalėdų!
[l^jɪŋks'mu: ka'l^je:du:!]

Happy New Year!
Sù Naujaìsiais mẽtais!
['sʊ nɑʊ'jʌɪs^jɛɪs 'm^jæetʌɪs!]

Happy Easter!
Sù Šventóm Velýkom!
['sʊ ʃv^jɛn'tom v^jɛ'l^ji:kom!]

Happy Hanukkah!
Sù Chanùka!
['sʊ xa'nʊka!]

I'd like to propose a toast.
Nóriu paskélbti tòstą.
['nor^jʊ pas'k^jɛl^jpt^jɪ 'tosta:.]

Cheers!
Į sveikãtą!
[i: sv^jɛɪ'ka:ta:!]

Let's drink to …!
Išgérkime ùž …!
[ɪʃg^jɛrk^jɪm^jɛ 'ʊʒ …!]

To our success!
Ùž mū̃sų sẽkmę!
['ʊʒ 'mu:su: 's^je:km^jɛ:!]

To your success!
Ùž jū̃sų sẽkmę!
['ʊʒ 'ju:su: 's^je:km^jɛ:!]

Good luck!
Sėkmẽs!
[s^je:k'm^je:s!]

Have a nice day!
Gẽros diẽnos!
['g^jẽros 'd^jɛnos!]

Have a good holiday!
Gerų̃ atóstogų!
[g^jɛ'ru: a'tostogu:!]

Have a safe journey!
Saũgios keliõnės!
['sɑʊg^jos ke'l^jo:n^je:s!]

I hope you get better soon!
Lìnkiu greĩtai pasveĩkti!
['l^jɪŋk^jʊ 'gr^jɛɪtʌɪ pas'v^jɛɪkt^jɪ!]

Socializing

Why are you sad?	**Kodėl táu liūdna?** [ko'dʲeːl 'tɑʊ lʲuːdʲna?]
Smile! Cheer up!	**Nusišypsók! Pralinksmék!** [nʊsʲɪʃɪːpʼsok! pralʲɪŋkʼsmʲeːk!]
Are you free tonight?	**Ar̃ jūs šiañdien neužsiẽmę?** [ar 'juːs 'ʃændʲiɛn neʊʒʼsʲɪeːmʲɛ:?]
May I offer you a drink?	**Ar̃ galiù táu pasiūlyti išgérti?** [ar ga'lʲʊ 'tɑʊ pa'sʲuːlʲiːtʲɪ iʃʼgʲɛrtʲɪ?]
Would you like to dance?	**Ar̃ norétum pašókti?** [ar noʼrʲeːtʊm paʼʃoktʲɪ?]
Let's go to the movies.	**Gál eĩkime į̃ kìną?** ['galʲ 'ɛɪkʲɪmʲɛ iː 'kʲɪːna:?]
May I invite you to ...?	**Ar̃ galiù tavè pakviẽsti ...?** [ar ga'lʲʊ ta'vʲɛ pak'vʲɛstʲɪ ...?]
a restaurant	**į̃ restorãną** [iː rʲɛstoʼra:naː]
the movies	**į̃ kìną** [iː 'kʲɪːna:]
the theater	**į̃ teãtrą** [iː tʲɛ'aːtraː]
go for a walk	**pasiváikščioti** [pasʲɪ'vʌɪkʃtsʲotʲɪ]
At what time?	**Kadà?** [ka'da?]
tonight	**šiąnakt** ['ʃæːnakt]
at six	**šẽštą** ['ʃæʃta:]
at seven	**septiñtą** [sʲɛpʼtʲɪnta:]
at eight	**aštuñtą** [aʃʼtʊnta:]
at nine	**deviñtą** [dʲɛ'vʲɪnta:]
Do you like it here?	**Ar̃ táu čià patiñka?** [ar 'tɑʊ tʂʲæ pa'tʲɪŋka?]
Are you here with someone?	**Ar̃ tù nè víena?** [ar 'tʊ nʲɛ 'vʲiena?]
I'm with my friend.	**Àš sù draugù /draugè/.** ['aʃ 'sʊ drɑʊ'gʊ /drɑʊ'gʲɛ/.]

I'm with my friends.	**Aš su draugaĩs /draugémìs/.** ['aʃ 'su drɑʊ'gʌɪs /drɑʊgʲe:'mʲɪs/.]
No, I'm alone.	**Nè, aš víena.** ['nʲɛ, aʃ 'vʲiɛna.]

Do you have a boyfriend?	**Ar̃ tùri vaikìną?** [ar 'tʊrʲɪ vʌɪ'kʲɪna:?]
I have a boyfriend.	**Turiù vaikìną.** [tʊ'rʲʊ vʌɪ'kʲɪna:.]
Do you have a girlfriend?	**Ar̃ tùri mergìną?** [ar 'tʊrʲɪ mʲɛr'gʲɪna:?]
I have a girlfriend.	**Turiù mergìną.** [tʊ'rʲʊ mʲɛr'gʲɪna:.]

Can I see you again?	**Ar̃ gãlime dár kadà pasimatýti?** [ar 'ga:lʲɪmʲɛ 'dar ka'da pasʲɪma'tʲi:tʲɪ?]
Can I call you?	**Ar̃ galiù táu paskam̃binti?** [ar ga'lʲʊ 'tɑʊ pas'kambʲɪntʲɪ?]
Call me. (Give me a call.)	**Paskam̃bink mán.** [pas'kambʲɪŋk 'man.]
What's your number?	**Kóks tàvo nùmeris?** ['koks 'tavʊ 'nʊmʲɛrʲɪs?]
I miss you.	**Pasìlgau tavę̃s.** [pasʲɪ'lʲgɑʊ ta'vʲɛ:s.]

You have a beautiful name.	**Tàvo gražùs var̃das.** ['tavʊ gra'ʒʊs 'vardas.]
I love you.	**Mýliu tavè.** ['mʲi:lʲʊ ta'vʲɛ.]
Will you marry me?	**Ar̃ tekési už manę̃s?** [ar te'kʲe:sʲɪ 'ʊʒ ma'nʲɛ:s?]
You're kidding!	**Tù juokáuji!** ['tʊ jʊɑ'kɑʊjɪ!]
I'm just kidding.	**Àš juokáuju.** ['aʃ jʊɑ'kɑʊjʊ.]

Are you serious?	**Ar̃ tù rimtaĩ?** [ar 'tʊ rʲɪm'tʌɪ?]
I'm serious.	**Àš rimtaĩ.** ['aʃ rʲɪm'tʌɪ.]
Really?!	**Tikraĩ?** [tʲɪk'rʌɪ?]
It's unbelievable!	**Neįtikétina!** [nʲɛɪ:tʲɪ'kʲe:tʲɪna!]
I don't believe you.	**Nètikiu.** ['nʲɛtʲɪkʲʊ.]
I can't.	**Àš negaliù.** ['aʃ nʲɛga'lʲʊ.]
I don't know.	**Nežinaũ.** [nʲɛʒʲɪ'nɑʊ.]
I don't understand you.	**Nesuprantù tavę̃s.** [nʲɛsʊpran'tʊ ta'vʲɛ:s.]

Please go away.

Prašau atstok.
[praˈʃɑʊ atsˈtok.]

Leave me alone!

Palìk manė víeną!
[paˈlʲɪk maˈnʲɛ ˈvʲiɛnaː!]

I can't stand him.

Àš negaliù jõ pakę̃st.
[ˈaʃ nʲɛgaˈlʲʊ jɔː paˈkʲɛːst.]

You are disgusting!

Tù šlykštùs!
[ˈtʊ ʃlʲiːkʃtʊs!]

I'll call the police!

Àš iškviēsiu polìciją!
[ˈaʃ iʃkʲvʲɛsʲʊ poˈlʲɪtsʲɪjaː!]

Sharing impressions. Emotions

I like it.	**Mán patiñka.**
	['man pa't^jɪŋka.]
Very nice.	**Labaì gražu.**
	[l^ja'bʌɪ gra'ʒʊ.]
That's great!	**Puikù!**
	[pʊi'kʊ!]
It's not bad.	**Neblogaì.**
	[n^jɛbl^jo'gʌɪ.]

I don't like it.	**Mán nepatiñka.**
	['man n^jɛpa't^jɪŋka.]
It's not good.	**Taì nėrà geraì.**
	['tʌɪ n^je:'ra ge'rʌɪ.]
It's bad.	**Taì blogaì.**
	['tʌɪ bl^jo'gʌɪ.]
It's very bad.	**Taì labaì blogaì.**
	['tʌɪ l^ja'bʌɪ bl^jo'gʌɪ.]
It's disgusting.	**Taì šlykštù.**
	[tʌɪ ʃl^ji:kʃ'tʊ.]

I'm happy.	**Àš laimìngas /laimìnga/.**
	['aʃ l^jʌɪ'm^jɪngas /l^jʌɪ'm^jɪnga/.]
I'm content.	**Àš paténkintas /paténkinta/.**
	['aʃ pa't^jɛŋk^jɪntas /pat^jɛŋk^jɪnta/.]
I'm in love.	**Àš įsimyléjęs /įsimyléjusi/.**
	['aʃ i:s^jɪm^jɪ:'l^je:jɛ:s /i:s^jɪm^jɪ:'l^je:jʊs^jɪ/.]
I'm calm.	**Àš ramùs /ramì/.**
	['aʃ ra'mʊs /ra'm^jɪ/.]
I'm bored.	**Mán nuobodù.**
	['man nʊɑbo'dʊ.]

I'm tired.	**Àš pavar̃gęs /pavar̃gusi/.**
	['aʃ pa'varg^jɛ:s /pa'vargʊs^jɪ/.]
I'm sad.	**Mán liūdnà.**
	['man 'l^ju:d'na.]
I'm frightened.	**Àš išsigañdęs /išsigañdusi/.**
	['aʃ iʃs^jɪ'gand^jɛ:s /iʃs^jɪ'gandʊs^jɪ/.]
I'm angry.	**Àš supỹkęs /supỹkusi/.**
	['aʃ sʊ'p^ji:k^jɛ:s /sʊ'p^ji:kʊs^jɪ/.]

I'm worried.	**Àš susirū̃pinęs /susirū̃pinusi/.**
	['aʃ sʊs^jɪ'ru:p^jɪn^jɛ:s /sʊs^jɪ'ru:p^jɪnʊs^jɪ/.]
I'm nervous.	**Àš susinèrvinęs /susinèrvinusi/.**
	['aʃ sʊs^jɪ'n^jɛrv^jɪn^jɛ:s /sʊs^jɪ'n^jɛrv^jɪnʊs^jɪ/.]

I'm jealous. (envious)

Àš pavýdžiu.
[ˈaʃ paˈvʲiːdʒʲʊ.]

I'm surprised.

Àš nustẽbęs /nustẽbusi/.
[ˈaʃ nʊstʲæbʲɛːs /nʊstʲæbusʲɪ/.]

I'm perplexed.

Àš sumìšęs /sumìšusi/.
[ˈaʃ sʊˈmʲɪʃɛːs /sʊˈmʲɪʃusʲɪ/.]

Problems. Accidents

I've got a problem.	**Atsitiko problema.** [atsʲɪ'tʲɪko problʲɛ'ma.]
We've got a problem.	**Mēs turime problemā.** ['mʲæs 'turʲɪmʲɛ problʲɛ'ma.]
I'm lost.	**Aš pasiklýdau.** ['aʃ pasʲɪk'lʲiːdɑʊ.]
I missed the last bus (train).	**Nespéjau į paskutìnį autobùsą (traukinį).** [nʲɛs'pʲeːljɛʊ iː pasku'tʲɪːnʲɪ: ɑʊto'busa: ('trɑʊkʲɪnʲɪː).]
I don't have any money left.	**Nebeturiù pinigų̃.** [nʲɛbʲɛtʊ'rʲʊ pʲɪnʲɪ'gu:.]
I've lost my ...	**Aš pàmečiau ...** ['aʃ 'pamʲɛtʃɛʊ ...]
Someone stole my ...	**Kažkàs pàvogé màno ...** [kaʒ'kas 'pavogʲe: 'manɔ ...]
passport	**pãsą** ['paːsa:]
wallet	**pinigìnę** [pʲɪnʲɪ'gʲɪnʲɛ:]
papers	**dokumentùs** [dokʊmʲɛn'tʊs]
ticket	**bìlietą** ['bʲɪlʲiɛta:]
money	**pìnigus** ['pʲɪnʲɪgʊs]
handbag	**rañkinę** ['raŋkʲɪnʲɛ:]
camera	**fotoaparãtą** [fotoapa'raːta:]
laptop	**nešiojamąjį kompiùterį** [nʲɛ'ʃojamaːjiː kom'pʲʊtʲɛrʲɪː]
tablet computer	**planšetinį kompiùterį** [plʲan'ʃɛtʲɪnʲɪː kom'pʲʊtʲɛrʲiː]
mobile phone	**mobilų̃jį telefòną** [mo'bʲɪlu:jiː tʲɛlʲɛ'fona:]
Help me!	**Padékite mán!** [pa'dʲeːkʲɪte 'man!]
What's happened?	**Kàs atsitìko?** ['kas atsʲɪ'tʲɪko?]

fire	**gaĩsras**
	['gʌɪsras]
shooting	**kažkàs šáudė**
	[kaʒ'kas 'ʃaʊdʲe:]
murder	**žmogžudỹstė**
	[ʒmogʒʊ'dʲi:stʲe:]
explosion	**sprogìmas**
	[spro'gʲɪmas]
fight	**muštỹnės**
	[mʊʃ'tʲi:nʲe:s]

Call the police!	**Kviẽskite polìciją!**
	['kvʲɛskʲɪtʲɛ po'lʲɪtsʲɪjaː!]
Please hurry up!	**Prašaũ, paskubékite!**
	[pra'ʃaʊ, paskʊ'bʲe:kʲɪte!]
I'm looking for the police station.	**Ieškau polìcijos skỹriaus.**
	['ɪɛʃkaʊ po'lʲɪtsɪjos 'skʲiːrʲɛʊs.]
I need to make a call.	**Mán reĩkia paskam̃binti.**
	['man 'rʲɛɪkʲɛ pas'kambʲɪntʲɪ.]
May I use your phone?	**Aȓ galiù pasinaudóti jū̃sų telefonù?**
	[ar ga'lʲʊ pasʲɪnaʊ'dotʲɪ 'juːsu: tʲɛlʲɛfo'nʊ?]

I've been …	**Manè …**
	[ma'nʲɛ …]
mugged	**apiplė́šė**
	[apʲɪ'plʲeːʃe:]
robbed	**àpvogė**
	['apvogʲe:]
raped	**išprievartãvo**
	[ɪʃprʲɪɛvar'ta:vo]
attacked (beaten up)	**užpúolė**
	[ʊʒ'pʊolʲe:]

Are you all right?	**Aȓ vìskas geraĩ?**
	[ar 'vʲɪskas gʲɛ'rʌɪ?]
Did you see who it was?	**Aȓ mãtėte, kàs taĩ bùvo?**
	[ar 'ma:tʲe:te, 'kas tʌɪ 'bʊvo?]
Would you be able to recognize the person?	**Aȓ sugebė́tumėte atpažìnti tą̃ žmogų?**
	[ar sʊge'bʲe:tʊmʲe:te atpa'ʒʲɪntʲɪ ta: 'ʒmogu:?]
Are you sure?	**Aȓ jū̃s tìkras /tikrà/?**
	[ar 'juːs tʲɪkras /tʲɪk'ra/?]

Please calm down.	**Prašaũ, nurìmkite.**
	[pra'ʃaʊ, nʊ'rʲɪmkʲɪtʲɛ.]
Take it easy!	**Ramiaũ!**
	[ra'mʲɛʊ!]
Don't worry!	**Nesijáudinkite!**
	[nʲɛsʲɪ'jaʊdʲɪŋkʲɪtʲɛ!]
Everything will be fine.	**Vìskas bùs geraĩ.**
	['vʲɪskas 'bʊs gʲɛ'rʌɪ.]

Everything's all right.	**Vìskas geraĩ.** ['vʲɪskas gʲɛ'rʌɪ.]
Come here, please.	**Prašaũ, ateĩkite čià.** [pra'ʃɑʊ, a'tʲɛɪkʲɪtʲɛ tʂʲæ.]
I have some questions for you.	**Turiù jùms kẽletą kláusimų.** [tʊ'rʲʊ 'jʊms 'kʲæɫʲɛta: 'klɑʊsʲɪmu:.]
Wait a moment, please.	**Prašaũ trupùtį paláukti.** [pra'ʃɑʊ trʊ'pʊtʲɪ: pa'lʲɑʊktʲɪ.]
Do you have any I.D.?	**Aȓ tùrite kokiùs noŕs asmeñs dokumentùs?** [ar 'tʊrʲɪtʲɛ ko'kʲʊs 'nors as'mʲɛns dokʊmʲɛn'tʊs?]
Thanks. You can leave now.	**Ãčiū. Gãlite eĩti.** ['a:tʂʲu:. 'ga:lʲɪtʲɛ 'ɛɪtʲɪ.]
Hands behind your head!	**Rankàs ùž galvõs!** [raŋ'kas 'ʊʒ galʲvo:s!]
You're under arrest!	**Jũs sùimamas!** ['ju:s 'sʊimamas!]

Health problems

Please help me.	**Prašaũ, padékite mán.** [pra'ʃɑʊ, padʲe:kʲɪte 'man.]
I don't feel well.	**Mán blogà.** ['man blʲo'ga.]
My husband doesn't feel well.	**Mãno výrui blogà.** ['ma:nɔ 'vʲi:rʊɪ blʲo'ga.]
My son ...	**Màno sūnui ...** ['manɔ 'su:nʊɪ ...]
My father ...	**Màno tévui ...** ['manɔ 'tʲe:vʊɪ ...]
My wife doesn't feel well.	**Màno žmónai blogà.** ['manɔ 'ʒmonʌɪ blʲo'ga.]
My daughter ...	**Màno dùkrai ...** ['manɔ 'dʊkrʌɪ ...]
My mother ...	**Màno mãmai ...** ['manɔ 'ma:mʌɪ ...]
I've got a ...	**Mán ...** ['man ...]
headache	**skaũda gálvą** ['skɑʊda 'galʲva:]
sore throat	**skaũda gérklę** ['skɑʊda 'gʲɛrklʲɛ:]
stomach ache	**skaũda skrañdį** ['skɑʊda 'skrandʲɪ:]
toothache	**skaũda dañtį** ['skɑʊda 'danti:]
I feel dizzy.	**Mán svaĩgsta galvà.** ['man 'svʌɪgsta galʲ'va.]
He has a fever.	**Jìs karščiúoja.** [jɪs karʃ'tsʲʊo:jɛ.]
She has a fever.	**Jì karščiúoja.** [jɪ karʃ'tsʲʊo:jɛ.]
I can't breathe.	**Negaliù kvépúoti.** [nʲɛga'lʲʊ kvʲe:'pʊotʲɪ.]
I'm short of breath.	**Mán sunkù kvépúoti.** ['man sʊŋ'kʊ kvʲe:'pʊotʲɪ.]
I am asthmatic.	**Sergù astmà.** [sʲɛr'gʊ ast'ma.]
I am diabetic.	**Sergù diabetù.** [sʲɛr'gʊ dʲæbʲɛ'tʊ.]

I can't sleep.	**Negaliu užmigti.** [nʲɛga'lʲʊ ʊʒ'mʲɪktʲɪ.]
food poisoning	**apsinuõdijimas maistu** [apsʲɪ'nʊadʲɪjimas mʌɪs'tʊ]

It hurts here.	**Skaũda čià.** ['skɑʊda 'tʂʲæ.]
Help me!	**Padékite mán!** [pa'dʲe:kʲɪte 'man!]
I am here!	**Àš čià!** ['aʃ tʂʲæ!]
We are here!	**Mẽs čià!** ['mʲæs tʂʲæ!]
Get me out of here!	**Ištráukite manè ìš čià!** [ɪʃ'trɑʊkʲɪtʲɛ ma'nʲɛ ɪʃ tʂʲæ!]
I need a doctor.	**Mán reìkia dãktaro.** ['man 'rʲɛɪkʲɛ 'da:ktarɔ.]
I can't move.	**Negaliu pajudéti.** [nʲɛga'lʲʊ pajʊ'dʲe:tʲɪ.]
I can't move my legs.	**Negaliu pajùdinti kójų.** [nʲɛga'lʲʊ pa'jʊdʲɪntʲɪ 'koju:.]

I have a wound.	**Àš sužeistas /sužeistà/.** ['aʃ 'sʊʒʲɛɪstas /sʊʒʲɛɪs'ta/.]
Is it serious?	**Ar̃ žaizdà sunkì?** [ar ʒʌɪz'da sʊŋ'kʲɪ?]
My documents are in my pocket.	**Mãno dokumeñtai kišenėje.** ['ma:nɔ dɔkʊ'mentʌɪ kʲɪ'ʃænʲe:je.]
Calm down!	**Nurìmkite!** [nʊrʲɪmkʲɪtʲɛ!]
May I use your phone?	**Ar̃ galiu pasinaudóti jū́sų telefonù?** [ar ga'lʲʊ pasʲɪnɑʊ'dotʲɪ 'ju:su: tʲɛlʲɛfo'nʊ?]

Call an ambulance!	**Kviẽskite greĩtają!** ['kvʲɛskʲɪtʲɛ 'grʲɛɪta:ja:!]
It's urgent!	**Taĩ skubù!** ['tʌɪ skʊ'bʊ!]
It's an emergency!	**Taĩ skubùs ãtvejis!** ['tʌɪ skʊ'bʊs 'a:tvʲɛjis!]
Please hurry up!	**Prašaũ, paskubékite!** [pra'ʃɑʊ, paskʊ'bʲe:kʲɪte!]
Would you please call a doctor?	**Ar̃ gãlite iškviẽsti dãktarą?** [ar 'ga:lʲɪtʲɛ iʃk'vʲɛstʲɪ 'da:ktara:?]
Where is the hospital?	**Kur̃ ligóninė?** ['kʊr lʲɪ'gonʲɪnʲe:?]

How are you feeling?	**Kaĩp jaũčiatės?** ['kʌɪp 'jɛʊtʂʲætʲe:s?]
Are you all right?	**Ar̃ vìskas geraĩ?** [ar 'vʲɪskas gʲɛ'rʌɪ?]
What's happened?	**Kàs atsitìko?** ['kas atsʲɪ'tʲɪko?]

I feel better now.	**Jaučiúosi geriaũ.** [jɛʊ'tʂʲʊosʲɪ gʲɛ'rʲɛʊ.]
It's OK.	**Vìskas tvarkojè.** ['vʲɪskas tvarko'jæ.]
It's all right.	**Vìskas geraĩ.** ['vʲɪskas gʲɛ'rʌɪ.]

At the pharmacy

pharmacy (drugstore)	**vaistinė** ['vʌɪstʲɪnʲeː]
24-hour pharmacy	**visą parą dirbanti vaistinė** ['vʲɪsɑː 'pɑːrɑː 'dʲɪrbantʲɪ 'vʌɪstʲɪnʲeː]
Where is the closest pharmacy?	**Kur yra artimiausia vaistinė?** ['kʊr iː'ra artʲɪ'mʲæusʲɛ 'vʌɪstʲɪnʲeː?]

Is it open now?	**Ar ji dabar dirba?** [ar jɪ da'bar 'dʲɪrba?]
At what time does it open?	**Kada ji atsidaro?** [ka'da jɪ atsʲɪ'daːro?]
At what time does it close?	**Kada ji užsidaro?** [ka'da jɪ ʊʒsʲɪ'daːro?]

Is it far?	**Ar ji toli?** [ar jɪ 'toːlʲɪ?]
Can I get there on foot?	**Ar galiu nueiti ten pėsčiomis?** [ar ga'lʲʊ 'nʊʲɛɪtʲɪ ten pʲeːstsʲo'mʲɪs?]
Can you show me on the map?	**Ar galite parodyti žemėlapyje?** [ar 'gaːlʲɪte pa'rodʲiːtʲɪ ʒe'mʲeːlapʲiːje?]

Please give me something for ...	**Duokite man kažką nuo ...** ['dʊokʲɪtʲɛ 'man kaʒ'ka: nʊɑ ...]
a headache	**galvos skausmo** [galʲ'voːs 'skɑʊsmɔ]
a cough	**kosulio** [kɔ'sʊlʲɔ]
a cold	**peršalimo** ['pʲɛrʃalʲɪmɔ]
the flu	**gripo** ['grʲɪpɔ]

a fever	**karščiavimo** [karʃ'tsʲævʲɪmɔ]
a stomach ache	**skrandžio skausmo** ['skrandʒʲɔ 'skɑʊsmɔ]
nausea	**pykinimo** ['pʲiːkʲɪnʲɪmɔ]
diarrhea	**viduriavimo** [vʲɪdʊ'rʲævʲɪmɔ]
constipation	**vidurių užkietėjimo** [vʲɪdʊ'rʲu: ʊʒkʲɪɛ'tʲɛjɪmɔ]
pain in the back	**nugaros skausmo** ['nʊgaros 'skɑʊsmɔ]

chest pain	**krutinės skausmo** [krʊtʲɪˈnʲeːs ˈskaʊsmɔ]
side stitch	**šóno diegìmo** [ˈʃɔnɔ dʲiɛˈɡʲɪmɔ]
abdominal pain	**pílvo skaūsmo** [ˈpʲɪlʲvɔ ˈskaʊsmɔ]

pill	**tablėtė** [tabˈlʲɛtʲeː]
ointment, cream	**tėpalas, krėmas** [ˈtʲæpalʲas, ˈkrʲɛmas]
syrup	**sìrupas** [ˈsʲɪrʊpas]
spray	**purškalas** [ˈpʊrʃkalʲas]
drops	**lašaì** [lʲaˈʃʌɪ]

You need to go to the hospital.	**Jùms reìkia į̃ ligóninę.** [ˈjʊms ˈrʲɛɪkʲɛ iː lʲɪˈɡonʲɪnʲɛː]
health insurance	**sveikãtos draudìmas** [svʲɛɪˈkaːtos draʊˈdʲɪmas]
prescription	**váisto recėptas** [ˈvʌɪstɔ rʲɛˈtsʲɛptas]
insect repellant	**vabzdžių̃ repeleñtas** [vabzˈdʒʲuː rʲɛpʲɛˈlʲɛntas]
Band Aid	**pleìstras** [ˈplʲɛɪstras]

The bare minimum

Excuse me, ...	**Atsiprašaū, ...** [atsʲɪpra'ʃɑʊ, ...]
Hello.	**Sveikì.** [svʲɛɪ'kʲɪ.]
Thank you.	**Āčiū.** ['a:tʃʲu:.]
Good bye.	**Ikì.** [ɪ'kʲɪ.]
Yes.	**Taĩp.** ['tʌɪp.]
No.	**Nè.** ['nʲɛ.]
I don't know.	**Nežinaū.** [nʲɛʒɪ'nɑʊ.]
Where? | Where to? | When?	**Kuȓ? | Kur? | Kadà?** ['kʊr? | 'kʊr? | ka'da?]
I need ...	**Mán reĩkia ...** ['man 'rʲɛɪkʲɛ ...]
I want ...	**Nóriu ...** ['norʲʊ ...]
Do you have ...?	**Aȓ tùrite ...?** [ar 'tʊrʲɪtʲɛ ...?]
Is there a ... here?	**Aȓ čià yrà ...?** [ar 'tʃʲæ i:'ra ...?]
May I ...?	**Aȓ galiù ...?** [ar ga'lʲʊ ...?]
..., please (polite request)	**Prašaū ...** [pra'ʃɑʊ ...]
I'm looking for ...	**Íeškau ...** ['ɪʲɛʃkɑʊ ...]
restroom	**tualèto** [tʊa'lʲɛtɔ]
ATM	**bankomãto** [baŋko'ma:tɔ]
pharmacy (drugstore)	**váistinės** ['vʌɪstʲɪnʲe:s]
hospital	**ligóninės** [lʲɪ'gonʲɪnʲe:s]
police station	**polìcijos skȳriaus** [po'lʲɪtsɪjɔs 'skʲi:rʲɛʊs]
subway	**metrò** [mʲɛ'tro]

taxi	**taksì** [tak'sʲɪ]
train station	**traukinių stotiės** [trɑʊkʲɪ'nʲu: sto'tʲɛs]

My name is ...	**Mãno vañdas ...** ['mɑːnɔ 'vardas ...]
What's your name?	**Kuõ jũs vardù?** ['kʊɑ 'juːs var'dʊ?]
Could you please help me?	**Atsiprašaũ, ař gãlite padéti?** [atsʲɪpra'ʃɑʊ, ar 'gɑːlʲɪte pa'dʲeːtʲɪ?]
I've got a problem.	**Atsitìko problemà.** [atsʲɪ'tʲɪkɔ problʲɛ'ma.]
I don't feel well.	**Mán blogà.** ['man blʲo'ga.]
Call an ambulance!	**Kviẽskite greĩtają!** ['kvʲɛskʲɪtʲɛ 'grʲɛɪta:ja:!]
May I make a call?	**Ař galiù paskambinti?** [ar ga'lʲʊ pas'kambʲɪntʲɪ?]

I'm sorry.	**Atsiprašaũ.** [atsʲɪpra'ʃɑʊ.]
You're welcome.	**Nėrà ùž kã.** [nʲeː'ra 'ʊʒ ka:.]

I, me	**àš** ['aʃ]
you (inform.)	**tù** ['tʊ]
he	**jìs** [jɪs]
she	**jì** [jɪ]
they (masc.)	**jiẽ** ['jiɛ]
they (fem.)	**jõs** ['jɔːs]
we	**mẽs** ['mʲæs]
you (pl)	**jũs** ['juːs]
you (sg, form.)	**Jũs** ['juːs]

ENTRANCE	**ĮĖJÌMAS** [iːʲɛː'jɪmas]
EXIT	**IŠĖJÌMAS** [ɪʃʲeː'jɪmas]
OUT OF ORDER	**NEVEĨKIA** [nʲɛ'vʲɛɪkʲɛ]
CLOSED	**UŽDARÝTA** [ʊʒda'rʲiːta]

OPEN   **ATIDARÝTA**
                        [atʲɪdaˈrʲiːta]

FOR WOMEN   **MÓTERŲ**
                        [ˈmotʲɛruː]

FOR MEN   **VÝRŲ**
                        [ˈvʲiːruː]

CONCISE DICTIONARY

This section contains more than 1,500 useful words arranged alphabetically. The dictionary includes a lot of gastronomic terms and will be helpful when ordering food at a restaurant or buying groceries

T&P Books Publishing

DICTIONARY CONTENTS

T&P Books Publishing

T&P Books Publishing

time	laĩkas (v)	['lʲʌɪkas]
hour	valandà (m)	[valʲan'da]
half an hour	pùsvalandis (v)	['pʊsvalʲandʲɪs]
minute	minùtė (m)	[mʲɪ'nutʲe:]
second	sekùndė (m)	[sʲɛ'kʊndʲe:]

today (adv)	šiañdien	['ʃændʲiɛn]
tomorrow (adv)	rytój	[rʲiː'toj]
yesterday (adv)	vãkar	['va:kar]

Monday	pirmãdienis (v)	[pʲɪr'ma:dʲiɛnʲɪs]
Tuesday	antrãdienis (v)	[an'tra:dʲiɛnʲɪs]
Wednesday	trečiãdienis (v)	[trʲɛ'tʃʲædʲiɛnʲɪs]
Thursday	ketvirtãdienis (v)	[kʲɛtvʲɪr'ta:dʲiɛnʲɪs]
Friday	penktãdienis (v)	[pʲɛŋk'ta:dʲiɛnʲɪs]
Saturday	šeštãdienis (v)	[ʃɛʃ'ta:dʲiɛnʲɪs]
Sunday	sekmãdienis (v)	[sʲɛk'ma:dʲiɛnʲɪs]

day	dienà (m)	[dʲiɛ'na]
working day	dárbo dienà (m)	['darbɔ dʲiɛ'na]
public holiday	šveñtinė dienà (m)	['ʃvɛntʲɪnʲe: dʲiɛ'na]
weekend	savaĩtgalis (v)	[sa'vʌɪtgalʲɪs]

week	savaĩtė (m)	[sa'vʌɪtʲe:]
last week (adv)	praeĩtą savaĩtę	['praʲɛɪta: sa'vʌɪtʲɛ:]
next week (adv)	ateĩnančią savaĩtę	[a'tʲɛɪnantʃʲæ: sa'vʌɪtʲɛ:]

sunrise	sáulės patekėjimas (v)	['sɑʊlʲe:s patʲɛ'kʲɛjɪmas]
sunset	saulėlydis (v)	[sɑʊ'lʲe:lʲi:dʲɪs]

in the morning	rytè	[rʲiː'tʲɛ]
in the afternoon	popiẽt	[pо'pʲɛt]

in the evening	vakarè	[vaka'rʲɛ]
tonight (this evening)	šiañdien vakarè	['ʃændʲiɛn vaka'rʲɛ]

at night	nãktį	['na:ktiː]
midnight	vidùrnaktis (v)	[vʲɪ'dʊrnaktʲɪs]

January	saũsis (v)	['sɑʊsʲɪs]
February	vasãris (v)	[va'sa:rʲɪs]
March	kovàs (v)	[kɔ'vas]
April	balañdis (v)	[ba'lʲandʲɪs]
May	gegužė̃ (m)	[gʲɛgʊ'ʒʲe:]
June	birželis (v)	[bʲɪr'ʒʲælʲɪs]

July	líepa (m)	['lʲiɛpa]
August	rugpjūtis (v)	[rʊg'pjuːtʲɪs]
September	rugséjis (v)	[rʊg'sʲɛjɪs]
October	spālis (v)	['spaːlʲɪs]
November	lápkritis (v)	['lʲaːpkrʲɪtʲɪs]
December	grúodis (v)	['grʊadʲɪs]
in spring	pavāsarį	[pa'vaːsarʲɪː]
in summer	vāsarą	['vaːsaraː]
in fall	rùdenį	['rʊdʲɛnʲɪː]
in winter	žiẽmą	['ʒʲɛmaː]
month	ménuo (v)	['mʲeːnʊa]
season (summer, etc.)	sezònas (v)	[sʲɛ'zonas]
year	mẽtai (v dgs)	['mʲætʌɪ]
century	ámžius (v)	['amʒʲʊs]

2. Numbers. Numerals

digit, figure	skaitmuõ (v)	[skʌɪt'mʊa]
number	skaĩčius (v)	['skʌɪtʂʲʊs]
minus sign	mìnusas (v)	['mʲɪnʊsas]
plus sign	pliùsas (v)	['plʲʊsas]
sum, total	sumà (m)	[sʊ'ma]
first (adj)	pìrmas	['pʲɪrmas]
second (adj)	añtras	['antras]
third (adj)	trẽčias	['trʲætʂʲæs]
0 zero	nùlis	['nʊlʲɪs]
1 one	víenas	['vʲiɛnas]
2 two	dù	['dʊ]
3 three	trìs	['trʲɪs]
4 four	keturì	[kʲɛtʊ'rʲɪ]
5 five	penkì	[pʲɛŋ'kʲɪ]
6 six	šešì	[ʃɛ'ʃɪ]
7 seven	septynì	[sʲɛptʲiː'nʲɪ]
8 eight	aštuonì	[aʃtʊa'nʲɪ]
9 nine	devynì	[dʲɛvʲiː'nʲɪ]
10 ten	dẽšimt	['dʲæʃɪmt]
11 eleven	vienúolika	[vʲiɛ'nʊalʲɪka]
12 twelve	dvýlika	['dvʲiːlʲɪka]
13 thirteen	trýlika	['trʲiːlʲɪka]
14 fourteen	keturiólika	[kʲɛtʊ'rʲolʲɪka]
15 fifteen	penkiólika	[pʲɛŋ'kʲolʲɪka]
16 sixteen	šešiólika	[ʃɛ'ʃolʲɪka]
17 seventeen	septyniólika	[sʲɛptʲiː'nʲolʲɪka]

| 18 eighteen | aštuoniólika | [aʃtuɑˈnʲolʲɪka] |
| 19 nineteen | devyniólika | [dʲɛvʲiːˈnʲolʲɪka] |

20 twenty	dvìdešimt	[ˈdvʲɪdʲɛʃɪmt]
30 thirty	trìsdešimt	[ˈtrʲɪsdʲɛʃɪmt]
40 forty	kéturiasdešim	[ˈkʲætʊrʲæsdʲɛʃɪmt]
50 fifty	peñkiasdešim	[ˈpʲɛŋkʲæsdʲɛʃɪmt]

60 sixty	šéšiasdešim	[ˈʃæʃæsdʲɛʃɪmt]
70 seventy	septýniasdešim	[sʲɛpˈtʲiːnʲæsdʲɛʃɪmt]
80 eighty	aštúoniasdešim	[aʃˈtuɑnʲæsdʲɛʃɪmt]
90 ninety	devýniasdešim	[dʲɛˈvʲiːnʲæsdʲɛʃɪmt]

100 one hundred	šim̃tas	[ˈʃɪmtas]
200 two hundred	dù šimtaĩ	[ˈdʊ ʃɪmˈtʌɪ]
300 three hundred	trìs šimtaĩ	[ˈtrʲɪs ʃɪmˈtʌɪ]
400 four hundred	keturì šimtaĩ	[kʲɛtʊˈrʲɪ ʃɪmˈtʌɪ]
500 five hundred	penkì šimtaĩ	[pʲɛŋˈkʲɪ ʃɪmˈtʌɪ]

600 six hundred	šešì šimtaĩ	[ʃɛˈʃɪ ʃɪmˈtʌɪ]
700 seven hundred	septynì šimtaĩ	[sʲɛpˈtʲiːnʲɪ ˈʃɪmtʌɪ]
800 eight hundred	aštuonì šimtaĩ	[aʃtuɑˈnʲɪ ʃɪmˈtʌɪ]
900 nine hundred	devynì šimtaĩ	[dʲɛvʲiːˈnʲɪ ʃɪmˈtʌɪ]
1000 one thousand	tū̃kstantis	[ˈtuːkstantʲɪs]

| 10000 ten thousand | dẽšimt tū̃kstančių | [ˈdʲæʃɪmt ˈtuːkstantʂʲuː] |
| one hundred thousand | šim̃tas tū̃kstančių | [ˈʃɪmtas ˈtuːkstantʂʲuː] |

| million | milijõnas (v) | [mʲɪlʲɪˈjɔːnas] |
| billion | milijárdas (v) | [mʲɪlʲɪˈjardas] |

3. Humans. Family

man (adult male)	výras (v)	[ˈvʲiːras]
young man	jaunuõlis (v)	[jɛʊˈnuɑlʲɪs]
teenager	paauglỹs (v)	[paɑʊˈglʲiːs]
woman	móteris (m)	[ˈmotʲɛrʲɪs]
girl (young woman)	panélė (m)	[paˈnʲælʲeː]

age	ámžius (v)	[ˈamʒʲʊs]
adult (adj)	suáugęs	[sʊˈɑʊgʲɛːs]
middle-aged (adj)	vidutìnio ámžiaus	[vʲɪdʊˈtʲɪnʲɔ ˈamʒʲɛʊs]
elderly (adj)	pagyvénęs	[pagʲiːˈvʲænʲɛːs]
old (adj)	sẽnas	[ˈsʲænas]

old man	sẽnis (v)	[ˈsʲænʲɪs]
old woman	sẽnė (m)	[ˈsʲænʲeː]
retirement	peñsija (m)	[ˈpʲɛnsʲɪjɛ]
to retire (from job)	išeĩti į peñsiją	[ɪˈʃɛɪtʲɪ iː ˈpʲɛnsʲɪjaː]
retiree	peñsininkas (v)	[ˈpʲɛnsʲɪnʲɪŋkas]

mother	mótina (m)	['motʲɪna]
father	tévas (v)	['tʲeːvas]
son	sūnùs (v)	[suːˈnʊs]
daughter	dukrà, duktě (m)	[dʊkˈra], [dʊkˈtʲeː]
brother	brólis (v)	['brolʲɪs]
elder brother	vyresnýsis brólis (v)	[vʲiːrʲɛsˈnʲiːsʲɪs 'brolʲɪs]
younger brother	jaunesnýsis brólis (v)	[jɛʊnʲɛsˈnʲiːsʲɪs 'brolʲɪs]
sister	sesuõ (m)	[sʲɛˈsʊɑ]
elder sister	vyresnióji sesuõ (m)	[vʲiːrʲɛsˈnʲoːjɪ sʲɛˈsʊɑ]
younger sister	jaunesnióji sesuõ (m)	[jɛʊnʲɛsˈnʲoːjɪ sʲɛˈsʊɑ]

parents	tévaĩ (v)	[tʲeːˈvʌɪ]
child	vaĩkas (v)	['vʌɪkas]
children	vaikaĩ (v)	[vʌɪˈkʌɪ]
stepmother	pãmotė (m)	['paːmotʲeː]
stepfather	patévis (v)	[paˈtʲeːvʲɪs]

grandmother	senẽlė (m)	[sʲɛˈnʲælʲeː]
grandfather	senẽlis (v)	[sʲɛˈnʲælʲɪs]
grandson	anũkas (v)	[aˈnuːkas]
granddaughter	anũkė (m)	[aˈnuːkʲeː]
grandchildren	anũkai (v)	[aˈnuːkʌɪ]
uncle	dẽdė (v)	['dʲeːdʲe]
aunt	tetà (m)	[tʲɛˈta]
nephew	sūnénas (v)	[suːˈnʲeːnas]
niece	dukteréčia (m)	[dʊktɛˈrʲeːtʂʲæ]

wife	žmonà (m)	[ʒmoˈna]
husband	výras (v)	['vʲiːras]
married (masc.)	vẽdęs	['vʲædʲɛːs]
married (fem.)	ištekéjusi	[ɪʃtɛˈkʲeːjʊsʲɪ]
widow	našlẽ (m)	[naʃˈlʲe]
widower	našlỹs (v)	[naʃˈlʲiːs]

| name (first name) | vaŕdas (v) | ['vardas] |
| surname (last name) | pavardě (m) | [pavarˈdʲeː] |

relative	gimináitis (v)	[gʲɪmʲɪˈnʌɪtʲɪs]
friend (masc.)	draũgas (v)	['drɑʊgas]
friendship	draugỹstė (m)	[drɑʊˈgʲiːstʲe]

partner	pártneris (v)	['partnʲɛrʲɪs]
superior (n)	viŕšininkas (v)	['vʲɪrʃɪnʲɪŋkas]
colleague	kolegà (v)	[kɔlʲɛˈga]
neighbors	kaimýnai (v)	[kʌɪˈmʲiːnʌɪ]

4. Human body

| organism (body) | organìzmas (v) | [orgaˈnʲɪzmas] |
| body | kũnas (v) | ['kuːnas] |

heart	širdìs (m)	[ʃɪr'dʲɪs]
blood	kraũjas (v)	['krɑʊjas]
brain	smẽgenys (v dgs)	['smʲægʲɛnʲi:s]
nerve	nèrvas (v)	['nʲɛrvas]

bone	káulas (v)	['kɑʊlʲas]
skeleton	griáučiai (v)	['grʲæʊtʂʲɛɪ]
spine (backbone)	stùburas (v)	['stʊbʊras]
rib	šónkaulis (v)	['ʃonkɑʊlʲɪs]
skull	káukolė (m)	['kɑʊkolʲe:]

muscle	raumuõ (v)	[rɑʊ'mʊɑ]
lungs	plaũčiai (v)	['plʲɑʊtʂʲɛɪ]
skin	óda (m)	['oda]

head	galvà (m)	[galʲ'va]
face	véidas (v)	['vʲɛɪdas]
nose	nósis (m)	['nosʲɪs]
forehead	kaktà (m)	[kak'ta]
cheek	skrúostas (v)	['skrʊɑstas]

mouth	burnà (m)	[bʊr'na]
tongue	liežùvis (v)	[lʲɛ'ʒʊvʲɪs]
tooth	dantìs (v)	[dan'tʲɪs]
lips	lū́pos (m dgs)	['lʲu:pos]
chin	smãkras (v)	['sma:kras]

ear	ausìs (m)	[ɑʊ'sʲɪs]
neck	kãklas (v)	['ka:klʲas]
throat	gerklė̃ (m)	[gʲɛrk'lʲe:]

eye	akìs (m)	[a'kʲɪs]
pupil	vyzdỹs (v)	[vʲi:z'dʲi:s]
eyebrow	añtakis (v)	['antakʲɪs]
eyelash	blakstíena (m)	[blʲak'stʲiɛna]

hair	plaukaĩ (v dgs)	[plʲɑʊ'kʌɪ]
hairstyle	šukúosena (m)	[ʃʊ'kʊɑsʲɛna]
mustache	ūsai (v dgs)	['u:sʌɪ]
beard	barzdà (m)	[barz'da]
to have (a beard, etc.)	nešióti	[nʲɛ'ʃʲotʲɪ]
bald (adj)	plìkas	['plʲɪkas]

hand	plãštaka (m)	['plʲa:ʃtaka]
arm	rankà (m)	[raŋ'ka]
finger	pir̃štas (v)	['pʲɪrʃtas]
nail	nãgas (v)	['na:gas]
palm	délnas (v)	['dʲɛlʲnas]

shoulder	petìs (v)	[pʲɛ'tʲɪs]
leg	kója (m)	['koja]
foot	pėdà (m)	[pʲe:'da]

| knee | kelias (v) | ['kʲælʲæs] |
| heel | kulnas (v) | ['kuʎnas] |

back	nugara (m)	['nʊgara]
waist	liemuo (v)	[lʲiɛ'mʊa]
beauty mark	apgamas (v)	['a:pgamas]
birthmark (café au lait spot)	apgamas (v)	['a:pgamas]

5. Medicine. Diseases. Drugs

health	sveikata (m)	[svʲɛɪka'ta]
well (not sick)	sveikas	['svʲɛɪkas]
sickness	liga (m)	[lʲɪ'ga]
to be sick	sirgti	['sʲɪrktʲɪ]
ill, sick (adj)	sergantis	['sʲɛrgantʲɪs]

cold (illness)	peršalimas (v)	['pʲɛrʃalʲɪmas]
to catch a cold	peršalti	['pʲɛrʃalʲtʲɪ]
tonsillitis	angina (m)	[angʲɪ'na]
pneumonia	plaučių uždegimas (v)	['plʲaʊtʃʲu: ʊʒdʲɛ'gʲɪmas]
flu, influenza	gripas (v)	['grʲɪpas]

runny nose (coryza)	sloga (m)	[slʲo'ga]
cough	kosulys (v)	[kɔsʊ'lʲi:s]
to cough (vi)	kosėti	['kosʲe:tʲɪ]
to sneeze (vi)	čiaudėti	['tʃʲæʊdʲe:tʲɪ]

stroke	insultas (v)	[ɪn'sʊlʲtas]
heart attack	infarktas (v)	[ɪn'farktas]
allergy	alergija (m)	[a'lʲɛrgʲɪjɛ]
asthma	astma (m)	[ast'ma]
diabetes	diabetas (v)	[dʲɪja'bʲɛtas]

tumor	auglys (v)	[aʊg'lʲi:s]
cancer	vėžys (v)	[vʲe:'ʒʲi:s]
alcoholism	alkoholizmas (v)	[alʲkoɣo'lʲɪzmas]
AIDS	ŽIV (v)	['ʒʲɪv]
fever	karštligė (m)	['karʃtlʲɪgʲe:]
seasickness	jūros liga (m)	['ju:ros lʲɪ'ga]

bruise (hématome)	mėlynė (m)	[mʲe:'lʲi:nʲe:]
bump (lump)	guzas (v)	['gʊzas]
to limp (vi)	šlubuoti	[ʃlʲʊ'bʊatʲɪ]
dislocation	išnirimas (v)	[ɪʃnʲɪ'rʲɪmas]
to dislocate (vt)	išnarinti	[ɪʃna'rʲɪntʲɪ]

fracture	lūžis (v)	['lʲu:ʒʲɪs]
burn (injury)	nudegimas (v)	[nʊdʲɛ'gʲɪmas]
injury	sužalojimas (v)	[sʊʒa'lʲo:jɪmas]

| pain, ache | skaũsmas (v) | ['skɑʊsmas] |
| toothache | dantų̃ skaũsmas (v) | [dan'tu: 'skɑʊsmas] |

to sweat (perspire)	prakaitúoti	[prakʌɪ'tʊɑtʲɪ]
deaf (adj)	kurčias	['kʊrtʃʲæs]
mute (adj)	nebylỹs	[nʲɛbʲiː'lʲiːs]

immunity	imunitètas (v)	[ɪmʊnʲɪ'tʲɛtas]
virus	vìrusas (v)	['vʲɪrʊsas]
microbe	mikróbas (v)	[mʲɪk'robas]
bacterium	baktèrija (m)	[bak'tʲɛrʲɪjɛ]
infection	infèkcija (m)	[ɪn'fʲɛktsʲɪjɛ]

hospital	ligóninė (m)	[lʲɪ'gonʲɪnʲeː]
cure	gýdymas (v)	['gʲiːdʲiːmas]
to vaccinate (vt)	skiẽpyti	['skʲɛpʲɪːtʲɪ]
to be in a coma	bū̃ti kõmoje	['buːtʲɪ 'kõmojɛ]
intensive care	reanimãcija (m)	[rʲɛanʲɪ'ma:tsʲɪjɛ]
symptom	simptõmas (v)	[sʲɪmp'tomas]
pulse	pùlsas (v)	['pʊlʲsas]

6. Feelings. Emotions. Conversation

I, me	àš	['aʃ]
you	tù	['tu]
he	jìs	[jɪs]
she	jì	[jɪ]

we	mẽs	['mʲæs]
you (to a group)	jū̃s	['juːs]
they	jiẽ	['jiɛ]

Hello! (fam.)	Sveĩkas!	['svʲɛɪkas!]
Hello! (form.)	Sveikì!	[svʲɛɪ'kʲɪ!]
Good morning!	Lãbas rýtas!	['lʲa:bas 'rʲiːtas!]
Good afternoon!	Labà dienà!	[lʲa'ba dʲiɛ'na!]
Good evening!	Lãbas vãkaras!	['lʲa:bas 'va:karas!]

to say hello	svéikintis	['svʲɛɪkʲɪntʲɪs]
to greet (vt)	svéikinti	['svʲɛɪkʲɪntʲɪ]
How are you?	Kaĩp sėkasi?	['kʌɪp 'sʲækasʲɪ?]
Bye-Bye! Goodbye!	Ikì pasimãtymo!	[ɪkʲɪ pasʲɪmatʲiː:mo!]
Thank you!	Ãčiū!	['a:tʃʲuː!]

feelings	jausmaĩ (v)	[jɛʊs'mʌɪ]
to be hungry	noréti válgyti	[no'rʲeːtʲɪ 'valʲgʲiː:tʲɪ]
to be thirsty	noréti gérti	[no'rʲeːtʲɪ 'gʲærtʲɪ]
tired (adj)	pavar̃gęs	[pa'vargʲɛ:s]
to be worried	jáudintis	['jɑʊdʲɪntʲɪs]
to be nervous	nèrvintis	['nʲɛrvʲɪntʲɪs]

hope	viltìs (m)	[vʲɪlʲˈtʲɪs]
to hope (vi, vt)	tikétis	[tʲɪˈkʲeːtʲɪs]

character	charãkteris (v)	[xaˈraːktʲɛrʲɪs]
modest (adj)	kuklùs	[kʊkˈlʲʊs]
lazy (adj)	tingùs	[tʲɪnˈɡʊs]
generous (adj)	dosnùs	[dosˈnʊs]
talented (adj)	talentìngas	[talʲɛnˈtʲɪngas]

honest (adj)	sąžinìngas	[saːʒʲɪˈnʲɪngas]
serious (adj)	rìmtas	[ˈrʲɪmtas]
shy, timid (adj)	drovùs	[droˈvʊs]
sincere (adj)	nuoširdùs	[nʊɑʃʲɪrˈdʊs]
coward	bailỹs (v)	[bʌɪˈlʲiːs]

to sleep (vi)	miegóti	[mʲiɛˈɡotʲɪ]
dream	sãpnas (v)	[ˈsaːpnas]
bed	lóva (m)	[ˈlʲova]
pillow	pagálvė (m)	[paˈɡalʲvʲeː]

insomnia	nẽmiga (m)	[ˈnʲæmʲɪga]
to go to bed	eĩti miegóti	[ˈɛɪtʲɪ mʲiɛˈɡotʲɪ]
nightmare	košmãras (v)	[koʃˈmaːras]
alarm clock	žadintùvas (v)	[ʒadʲɪnˈtʊvas]

smile	šỹpsena (m)	[ˈʃʲiːpsʲɛna]
to smile (vi)	šypsótis	[ʃʲiːpˈsotʲɪs]
to laugh (vi)	juõktis	[ˈjuɑktʲɪs]

quarrel	bãrnis (v)	[ˈbarnʲɪs]
insult	įžeidìmas (v)	[iːʒʲɛɪˈdʲiːmas]
resentment	núoskauda (m)	[ˈnʊɑskɑʊda]
angry (mad)	pìktas	[ˈpʲɪktas]

7. Clothing. Personal accessories

clothes	aprangà (m)	[apranˈga]
coat (overcoat)	páltas (v)	[ˈpalʲtas]
fur coat	kailiniaĩ (v dgs)	[kʌɪlʲɪˈnʲɪɛɪ]
jacket (e.g., leather ~)	striùkė (m)	[ˈstrʲʊkʲeː]
raincoat (trenchcoat, etc.)	apsiaũstas (v)	[apˈsʲɛʊstas]

shirt (button shirt)	marškiniaĩ (v dgs)	[marʃˈkʲɪrʲnʲɛɪ]
pants	kélnės (m dgs)	[ˈkʲɛlʲnʲeːs]
suit jacket	švarˉkas (v)	[ˈʃvarkas]
suit	kostiùmas (v)	[kosˈtʲʊmas]
dress (frock)	suknélė (m)	[sʊkˈnʲælʲeː]
skirt	sijõnas (v)	[sʲɪˈjɔːnas]
T-shirt	futbolininko marškiniaĩ (v)	[ˈfʊtbolʲɪnʲɪŋkɔ marʃˈkʲɪrʲnʲɛɪ]

bathrobe	chalãtas (v)	[xaˈlʲaːtas]
pajamas	pižamà (m)	[pʲɪʒaˈma]
workwear	dárbo drabùžiai (v)	[ˈdarbɔ draˈbʊʒʲɛɪ]

underwear	baltiniaĩ (v dgs)	[balʲtʲɪˈnʲɛɪ]
socks	kójinės (m dgs)	[ˈkoːjɪnʲeːs]
bra	liemenė̃lė (m)	[lʲiɛmeˈnʲeːlʲeː]
pantyhose	pėdkelnės (m dgs)	[ˈpʲeːdkʲɛlʲnʲeːs]
stockings (thigh highs)	kójinės (m dgs)	[ˈkoːjɪnʲeːs]
bathing suit	máudymosi kostiumė̃lis (v)	[ˈmɑʊdʲiːmosʲɪ kostʲʊˈmʲeːlʲɪs]

hat	kepùrė (m)	[kʲɛˈpʊrʲeː]
footwear	ãvalynė (m)	[ˈaːvalʲɪːnʲeː]
boots (e.g., cowboy ~)	aulìniai bãtai (v)	[ɑʊˈlʲɪnʲɛɪ ˈbaːtʌɪ]
heel	kùlnas (v)	[ˈkʊlʲnas]
shoestring	bãtraištis (v)	[ˈbaːtrʌɪʃtʲɪs]
shoe polish	ãvalynė̃s krèmas (v)	[ˈaːvalʲɪːnʲeːs ˈkrʲɛmas]

cotton (n)	mẽdvilnė (m)	[ˈmʲædvʲɪlʲnʲeː]
wool (n)	vìlna (m)	[ˈvʲɪlʲna]
fur (n)	káilis (v)	[ˈkʌɪlʲɪs]

gloves	pìrštinės (m dgs)	[ˈpʲɪrʃtʲɪnʲeːs]
mittens	kùmštinės (m dgs)	[ˈkʊmʃtʲɪnʲeːs]
scarf (muffler)	šãlikas (v)	[ˈʃaːlʲɪkas]
glasses (eyeglasses)	akiniaĩ (dgs)	[akʲɪˈnʲɛɪ]
umbrella	skė̃tis (v)	[ˈskʲeːtʲɪs]
tie (necktie)	kaklãraištis (v)	[kakˈlʲaːrʌɪʃtʲɪs]
handkerchief	nósinė (m)	[ˈnosʲɪnʲeː]
comb	šùkos (m dgs)	[ˈʃʊkos]
hairbrush	plaukų̃ šepetỹs (v)	[plʲɑʊˈku: ʃɛpʲɛˈtʲiːs]

buckle	sagtìs (m)	[sakˈtʲɪs]
belt	dìržas (v)	[ˈdʲɪrʒas]
purse	rankinùkas (v)	[raŋkʲɪˈnʊkas]

collar	apýkaklė (m)	[aˈpʲiːkaklʲeː]
pocket	kišẽnė (m)	[kʲɪˈʃænʲeː]
sleeve	rankóvė (m)	[raŋˈkovʲeː]
fly (on trousers)	klỹnas (v)	[ˈklʲiːnas]

zipper (fastener)	užtrauktùkas (v)	[ʊʒtrɑʊkˈtʊkas]
button	sagà (m)	[saˈga]
to get dirty (vi)	išsitèpti	[ɪʃsʲɪˈtʲɛptʲɪ]
stain (mark, spot)	dė́mė (m)	[dʲeːˈmʲeː]

8. City. Urban institutions

store	parduotùvė (m)	[pardʊɑˈtʊvʲeː]
shopping mall	prekýbos ceñtras (v)	[prʲɛˈkʲiːbos ˈtsʲɛntras]

supermarket	supermárketas (v)	[sʊpⁱɛr'markⁱɛtas]
shoe store	ávalynės parduotùvė (m)	['a:valⁱi:nⁱe:s pardʊa'tʊvⁱe:]
bookstore	knygýnas (v)	[knⁱi:'gⁱi:nas]

drugstore, pharmacy	váistinė (m)	['vʌistⁱInⁱe:]
bakery	bandẽlių kráutuvė (m)	[ban'dⁱælⁱu: 'krautʊvⁱe:]
pastry shop	konditérija (m)	[kondⁱI'tⁱɛrⁱIjɛ]
grocery store	bakaléja (m)	[baka'lⁱe:ja]
butcher shop	mėsõs kráutuvė (m)	[mⁱe:'so:s 'krautʊvⁱe:]
produce store	daržóvių kráutuvė (m)	[dar'ʒovⁱu: 'krautʊvⁱe:]
market	prekývietė (m)	[prⁱɛ'kⁱi:vⁱiɛtⁱe:]

hair salon	kirpyklà (m)	[kⁱIrpⁱi:k'lⁱa]
post office	pãštas (v)	['pa:ʃtas]
dry cleaners	valyklà (m)	[valⁱi:k'la]
circus	cìrkas (v)	['tsⁱIrkas]
zoo	zoológijos sõdas (v)	[zoo'lⁱogⁱIjos 'so:das]

theater	teãtras (v)	[tⁱɛ'a:tras]
movie theater	kìno teãtras (v)	['kⁱIno tⁱɛ'a:tras]
museum	muziẽjus (v)	[mʊ'zⁱɛjʊs]
library	bibliotekà (m)	[bⁱIblⁱIjotⁱɛ'ka]

mosque	mečẽtė (m)	[mⁱɛ'tsⁱɛtⁱe:]
synagogue	sinagogà (m)	[sⁱInago'ga]
cathedral	kãtedra (m)	['ka:tⁱɛdra]
temple	šventyklà (m)	[ʃvⁱɛntⁱi:k'lⁱa]
church	bažnýčia (m)	[baʒ'nⁱi:tʂⁱæ]

college	institùtas (v)	[Instⁱ'I'tʊtas]
university	universitètas (v)	[ʊnⁱIvⁱɛrsⁱI'tⁱɛtas]
school	mokyklà (m)	[mokⁱi:k'lⁱa]

hotel	viẽšbutis (v)	['vⁱɛʃbʊtⁱIs]
bank	bánkas (v)	['baŋkas]
embassy	ambasadà (m)	[ambasa'da]
travel agency	turìzmo agentūrà (m)	[tʊ'rⁱIzmo agⁱɛntu:'ra]

subway	metrò	[mⁱɛ'tro]
hospital	ligóninė (m)	[lⁱI'gonⁱInⁱe:]
gas station	degalìnė (m)	[dⁱɛga'lⁱInⁱe:]
parking lot	stovéjimo aikštẽlė (m)	[sto'vⁱɛjImo ʌIkʃ'tⁱælⁱe:]

ENTRANCE	ĮĖJÌMAS	[i:ⁱɛ:'jImas]
EXIT	IŠĖJÌMAS	[Iʃⁱe:'jImas]
PUSH	STÙMTI	['stʊmtⁱI]
PULL	TRÁUKTI	['traʊktⁱI]
OPEN	ATIDARÝTA	[atⁱIda'rⁱi:ta]
CLOSED	UŽDARÝTA	[ʊʒda'rⁱi:ta]

| monument | pamiñklas (v) | [pa'mⁱIŋklⁱas] |
| fortress | tvirtóvė (m) | [tvⁱIr'tovⁱe:] |

palace	rū́mai (v)	['ru:mʌɪ]
medieval (adj)	vidùramžių	[vʲɪ'dʊramʒʲu:]
ancient (adj)	senóvinis	[sʲɛ'novʲɪnʲɪs]
national (adj)	nacionãlinis	[natsʲɪjɔ'na:lʲɪnʲɪs]
famous (monument, etc.)	žymùs	[ʒʲi:'mʊs]

9. Money. Finances

money	pinigaĩ (v)	[pʲɪnʲɪ'gʌɪ]
coin	monetà (m)	[monʲɛ'ta]
dollar	dóleris (v)	['dolʲɛrʲɪs]
euro	eūras (v)	['ɛʊras]

ATM	bankomãtas (v)	[baŋko'ma:tas]
currency exchange	keityklà (m)	[kʲɛɪtʲi:k'lʲa]
exchange rate	kùrsas (v)	['kʊrsas]
cash	gryníeji pinigaĩ (v)	[grʲi:'nʲiɛjɪ pʲɪnʲɪ'gʌɪ]

How much?	Kíek?	['kʲiɛk?]
to pay (vi, vt)	mokéti	[mo'kʲe:tʲɪ]
payment	apmokéjimas (v)	[apmo'kʲɛjɪmas]
change (give the ~)	grąžà (m)	[gra:'ʒa]

price	kaina (m)	['kʌɪna]
discount	núolaida (m)	['nʊalʌɪda]
cheap (adj)	pigùs	[pʲɪ'gʊs]
expensive (adj)	brangùs	[bran'gʊs]

bank	bánkas (v)	['baŋkas]
account	są́skaita (m)	['sa:skʌɪta]
credit card	kredìtinė kortēlė (m)	[krʲɛ'dʲɪtʲɪnʲe: kor'tʲælʲe:]
check	čēkis (v)	['tʂʲɛkʲɪs]
to write a check	išrašýti čēkį	[ɪʂra'ʃʲɪ:tʲɪ 'tʂʲɛkʲɪ:]
checkbook	čēkių knygēlė (m)	['tʂʲɛkʲu: knʲi:'gʲælʲe:]

debt	skolà (m)	[sko'lʲa]
debtor	skólininkas (v)	['sko:lʲɪnʲɪŋkas]
to lend (money)	dúoti į̃ skõlą	['dʊatʲɪ i: 'sko:lʲa:]
to borrow (vi, vt)	im̃ti į̃ skõlą	['ɪmtʲɪ i: 'sko:lʲa:]

to rent (~ a tuxedo)	išsinúomoti	[ɪʃsʲɪ'nʊamotʲɪ]
on credit (adv)	kreditù	[krʲɛdʲɪ'tʊ]
wallet	piniginė (m)	[pʲɪnʲɪ'gʲɪnʲe:]
safe	seĩfas (v)	['sʲɛɪfas]
inheritance	palikìmas (v)	[palʲɪ'kʲɪmas]
fortune (wealth)	tùrtas (v)	['tʊrtas]

tax	mókestis (v)	['mokʲɛstʲɪs]
fine	baudà (m)	[baʊ'da]
to fine (vt)	baũsti	['baʊstʲɪ]

wholesale (adj)	didmenìnis	[dʲɪdmʲɛ'nʲɪnʲɪs]
retail (adj)	mažmenìnis	[maʒmʲɛ'nʲɪnʲɪs]
to insure (vt)	draũsti	['drɑʊstʲɪ]
insurance	draudìmas (v)	[drɑʊ'dʲɪmas]

capital	kapitãlas (v)	[kapʲɪ'ta:lʲas]
turnover	apývarta (m)	[a'pʲi:varta]
stock (share)	ãkcija (m)	['a:ktsʲɪjɛ]
profit	pelnas (v)	['pʲɛlˠnas]
profitable (adj)	pelnìngas	[pʲɛlʲⁱnʲɪngas]

crisis	krìzė (m)	['krʲɪzʲe:]
bankruptcy	bankròtas (v)	[baŋk'rotas]
to go bankrupt	bankrutúoti	[baŋkrʊ'tʊɑtʲɪ]

accountant	buháfteris (v)	[bʊ'ɣalʲtʲɛrʲɪs]
salary	dárbo ùžmokestis (v)	['darbɔ 'ʊʒmokʲɛstʲɪs]
bonus (money)	premija (m)	['prʲɛmʲɪjɛ]

10. Transportation

bus	autobùsas (v)	[ɑʊto'bʊsas]
streetcar	tramvãjus (v)	[tram'va:jʊs]
trolley bus	troleibùsas (v)	[trolʲɛɪ'bʊsas]

to go by ...	važiúoti ...	[va'ʒʲʊɑtʲɪ ...]
to get on (~ the bus)	įlìpti į̃ ...	[i:'lʲɪ:ptʲɪ i: ...]
to get off ...	išlìpti ìš ...	[ɪʃlʲⁱɪptʲɪ ɪʃ ...]

stop (e.g., bus ~)	stotėlė (m)	[sto'tʲælʲe:]
terminus	galutìnė stotėlė (m)	[galʊ'tʲɪnʲe: sto'tʲælʲe:]
schedule	tvarkãraštis (v)	[tvar'ka:raʃtʲɪs]
ticket	bìlietas (v)	['bʲɪlʲⁱietas]
to be late (for ...)	vėlúoti	[vʲe:'lʲʊɑtʲɪ]

taxi, cab	taksì (v)	[tak'sʲɪ]
by taxi	sù taksì	['sʊ tak'sʲɪ]
taxi stand	taksì stovėjimo aikštėlė (m)	[tak'sʲɪ sto'vʲɛjɪmɔ ʌɪkʃ'tʲælʲe:]

traffic	gãtvės judėjimas (v)	['ga:tvʲe:s jʊ'dʲɛjɪmas]
rush hour	pìko vãlandos (m dgs)	['pʲɪkɔ 'va:lʲandos]
to park (vi)	parkúotis	[par'kʊɑtʲɪs]

subway	metrò	[mʲɛ'tro]
station	stotìs (m)	[sto'tʲɪs]
train	traukinỹs (v)	[trɑʊkʲɪ'nʲi:s]
train station	stotìs (m)	[sto'tʲɪs]
rails	bėgiai (v dgs)	['bʲe:gʲɛɪ]
compartment	kupė (m)	[kʊ'pʲe:]

berth	lentýna (m)	[lʲɛnˈtʲiːna]
airplane	léktuvas (v)	[lʲeːkˈtʊvas]
air ticket	léktuvo bìlietas (v)	[lʲeːkˈtʊvɔ ˈbʲɪlʲiɛtas]
airline	aviakompãnija (m)	[avʲækomˈpaːnʲɪjɛ]
airport	óro úostas (v)	[ˈorɔ ˈʊɑstas]

flight (act of flying)	skrýdis (v)	[ˈskrʲiːdʲɪs]
luggage	bagãžas (v)	[baˈgaːʒas]
luggage cart	vežimẽlis (v)	[vʲɛʒˈɪˈmʲeːlʲɪs]

ship	laĩvas (v)	[ˈlʲʌɪvas]
cruise ship	láineris (v)	[ˈlʲʌɪnʲɛrʲɪs]
yacht	jachtà (m)	[jaxˈta]
boat (flat-bottomed ~)	váltis (m)	[ˈvalʲtʲɪs]

captain	kapitõnas (v)	[kapʲɪˈtoːnas]
cabin	kajùtė (m)	[kaˈjʊtʲeː]
port (harbor)	úostas (v)	[ˈʊɑstas]

bicycle	dvìratis (v)	[ˈdvʲɪratʲɪs]
scooter	motoróleris (v)	[motoˈrolʲɛrʲɪs]
motorcycle, bike	motocìklas (v)	[motoˈtsʲɪklʲas]
pedal	pedãlas (v)	[pʲɛˈdaːlʲas]
pump	siurblýs (v)	[sʲʊrˈblʲiːs]
wheel	rãtas (v)	[ˈraːtas]

automobile, car	automobìlis (v)	[ɑʊtomoˈbʲɪlʲɪs]
ambulance	greitóji pagálba (m)	[grʲɛɪˈtoːjɪ paˈgalʲba]
truck	suñkvežimis (v)	[ˈsʊŋkvʲɛʒʲɪmʲɪs]
used (adj)	dėvétas	[dʲeːˈvʲeːtas]
car crash	avãrija (m)	[aˈvaːrʲjɛ]
repair	remóntas (v)	[rʲɛˈmontas]

11. Food. Part 1

meat	mėsà (m)	[mʲeːˈsa]
chicken	vištà (m)	[vʲɪʃˈta]
duck	ántis (m)	[ˈantʲɪs]

pork	kiaulíena (m)	[kʲɛʊˈlʲiɛna]
veal	veršíena (m)	[vʲɛrˈʃiɛna]
lamb	avíena (m)	[aˈvʲiɛna]
beef	jáutiena (m)	[ˈjɑʊtʲiɛna]

| sausage (bologna, pepperoni, etc.) | dešrà (m) | [dʲɛʃˈra] |

egg	kiaušìnis (v)	[kʲɛʊˈʃɪnʲɪs]
fish	žuvìs (m)	[ʒʊˈvʲɪs]
cheese	sū̃ris (v)	[ˈsuːrʲɪs]
sugar	cùkrus (v)	[ˈtsʊkrʊs]

salt	druska (m)	[drʊs'ka]
rice	rỹžiai (v)	['rʲiːʒʲɛɪ]
pasta (macaroni)	makaronai (v dgs)	[maka'roːnʌɪ]
butter	svíestas (v)	['svʲiɛstas]
vegetable oil	augalìnis aliẽjus (v)	[ɑʊgalʲɪnʲɪs a'lʲɛjʊs]
bread	dúona (m)	['dʊɑna]
chocolate (n)	šokoládas (v)	[ʃoko'lʲaːdas]

wine	vỹnas (v)	['vʲiːnas]
coffee	kavà (m)	[ka'va]
milk	píenas (v)	['pʲiɛnas]
juice	sùltys (m dgs)	['sʊlʲtʲiːs]
beer	alùs (v)	[a'lʲʊs]
tea	arbatà (m)	[arba'ta]

tomato	pomidòras (v)	[pomʲɪ'doras]
cucumber	agùrkas (v)	[a'gʊrkas]
carrot	morkà (m)	[mor'ka]
potato	bùlvė (m)	['bʊlʲvʲeː]
onion	svogū́nas (v)	[svo'guːnas]
garlic	česnãkas (v)	[tɕʲɛs'naːkas]

cabbage	kopū́stas (v)	[kɔ'puːstas]
beetroot	runkelis, burõkas (v)	['rʊŋkʲɛlʲɪs], [bʊ'roːkas]
eggplant	baklažãnas (v)	[baklʲa'ʒaːnas]
dill	krãpas (v)	['kraːpas]
lettuce	salóta (m)	[sa'lʲoːta]
corn (maize)	kukurū́zas (v)	[kʊkʊ'ruːzas]

fruit	vaĩsius (v)	['vʌɪsʲʊs]
apple	obuolỹs (v)	[obʊa'lʲiːs]
pear	kriáušė (m)	['krʲæʊʃʲeː]
lemon	citrinà (m)	[tsʲɪtrʲɪ'na]
orange	apelsìnas (v)	[apʲɛlʲʲsʲɪnas]
strawberry (garden ~)	brãškė (m)	['braːʃkʲeː]

plum	slyvà (m)	[slʲiːʲva]
raspberry	aviẽtė (m)	[a'vʲɛtʲeː]
pineapple	ananãsas (v)	[ana'naːsas]
banana	banãnas (v)	[ba'naːnas]
watermelon	arbū́zas (v)	[ar'buːzas]
grape	vỹnuogės (m dgs)	['vʲiːnʊagʲeːs]
melon	meliònas (v)	[mʲɛ'lʲonas]

12. Food. Part 2

cuisine	virtùvė (m)	[vʲɪr'tʊvʲeː]
recipe	recèptas (v)	[rʲɛ'tsʲɛptas]
food	valgis (v)	['valʲgʲɪs]
to have breakfast	pùsryčiauti	['pʊsrʲiːtɕʲɛʊtʲɪ]

to have lunch	pietáuti	[pʲiɛ'tɑʊtʲɪ]
to have dinner	vakarieniáuti	[vakarʲiɛ'nʲæʊtʲɪ]
taste, flavor	skõnis (v)	['sko:nʲɪs]
tasty (adj)	skanùs	[ska'nʊs]
cold (adj)	šáltas	['ʃalʲtas]
hot (adj)	kárštas	['karʃtas]
sweet (sugary)	saldùs	[salʲ'dʊs]
salty (adj)	sūrùs	[su:'rʊs]
sandwich (bread)	sumuštìnis (v)	[sʊmʊʃ'tʲɪnʲɪs]
side dish	garnỹras (v)	[gar'nʲi:ras]
filling (for cake, pie)	ĩdaras (v)	['i:daras]
sauce	pãdažas (v)	['pa:daʒas]
piece (of cake, pie)	gãbalas (v)	['ga:balʲas]
diet	dietà (m)	[dʲiɛ'ta]
vitamin	vitamìnas (v)	[vʲɪta'mʲɪnas]
calorie	kalòrija (m)	[ka'lʲorʲɪjɛ]
vegetarian (n)	vegetãras (v)	[vʲɛgʲɛ'ta:ras]
restaurant	restorãnas (v)	[rʲɛsto'ra:nas]
coffee house	kavìnė (m)	[ka'vʲɪnʲe:]
appetite	apetìtas (v)	[apʲɛ'tʲɪtas]
Enjoy your meal!	Gẽro apetìto!	['gʲæro apʲɛ'tʲɪto!]
waiter	padavéjas (v)	[pada'vʲe:jas]
waitress	padavéja (m)	[pada'vʲe:ja]
bartender	bármenas (v)	['barmʲɛnas]
menu	meniù (v)	[mʲɛ'nʲu]
spoon	šáukštas (v)	['ʃɑʊkʃtas]
knife	peĩlis (v)	['pʲɛɪlʲɪs]
fork	šakùtė (m)	[ʃa'kʊtʲe:]
cup (e.g., coffee ~)	puodùkas (v)	[pʊɑ'dʊkas]
plate (dinner ~)	lėkštė̃ (m)	[lʲe:kʃ'tʲe:]
saucer	lėkštẽlė (m)	[lʲe:kʃ'tʲælʲe:]
napkin (on table)	servetė̃lė (m)	[sʲɛrvʲe'tʲe:lʲe:]
toothpick	dantų̃ krapštùkas (v)	[dan'tu: krapʃ'tʊkas]
to order (meal)	užsisakýti	[ʊʒsʲɪsakʲi:tʲɪ]
course, dish	pãtiekalas (v)	['pa:tʲiɛkalʲas]
portion	pòrcija (m)	['portsʲɪjɛ]
appetizer	ùžkandis (v)	['ʊʒkandʲɪs]
salad	salõtos (m)	[sa'lʲo:tos]
soup	sriubà (m)	[srʲʊ'ba]
dessert	desèrtas (v)	[dʲɛ'sʲɛrtas]
jam (whole fruit jam)	uogíenė (m)	[ʊɑ'gʲɛnʲe:]
ice-cream	ledaĩ (v dgs)	[lʲɛ'dʌɪ]
check	sąskaita (m)	['sa:skʌɪta]

| to pay the check | apmokéti sąskaitą | [apmo'kʲe:tʲɪ 'sa:skʌɪta:] |
| tip | arbãtpinigiai (v dgs) | [ar'ba:tpʲɪnʲɪgʲɛɪ] |

13. House. Apartment. Part 1

house	nãmas (v)	['na:mas]
country house	užmiesčio nãmas (v)	['ʊʒmʲiɛstsʲɔ 'na:mas]
villa (seaside ~)	vilà (m)	[vʲɪ'lʲa]

floor, story	aũkštas (v)	['ɑʊkʃtas]
entrance	láiptinė (m)	['lʲʌɪptʲɪnʲe:]
wall	síena (m)	['sʲiɛna]
roof	stógas (v)	['stogas]
chimney	vamzdis (v)	['vamzdʲɪs]

attic (storage place)	palépė (m)	[pa'lʲe:pʲe:]
window	langas (v)	['lʲangas]
window ledge	palángė (m)	[pa'lʲangʲe:]
balcony	balkonas (v)	[balʲ'konas]

stairs (stairway)	láiptai (v dgs)	['lʲʌɪptʌɪ]
mailbox	pãšto dėžutė (m)	['pa:ʃtɔ dʲe:'ʒʊtʲe:]
garbage can	šiukšlių bãkas (v)	['ʃʊkʃlʲu: 'ba:kas]
elevator	liftas (v)	['lʲɪftas]

electricity	elektrà (m)	[ɛlʲɛkt'ra]
light bulb	lemputė (m)	[lʲɛm'pʊtʲe:]
switch	jungiklis (v)	[jʊn'gʲɪklʲɪs]
wall socket	šakutės lizdas (v)	[ʃa'kʊtʲe:s 'lʲɪzdas]
fuse	saugiklis (v)	[sɑʊ'gʲɪklʲɪs]

door	durys (m dgs)	['dʊrʲi:s]
handle, doorknob	rañkena (m)	['raŋkʲɛna]
key	rãktas (v)	['ra:ktas]
doormat	kilimas (v)	['kʲɪlʲɪmas]

door lock	spynà (m)	[spʲɪ'na]
doorbell	skambutis (v)	[skam'bʊtʲɪs]
knock (at the door)	beldimas (v)	[bʲɛlʲ'dʲɪmas]
to knock (vi)	baladóti	[balʲa'dotʲɪ]
peephole	akutė (m)	[a'kʊtʲe:]

yard	kiemas (v)	['kʲɛmas]
garden	sódas (v)	['so:das]
swimming pool	baseinas (v)	[ba'sʲɛɪnas]
gym (home gym)	spòrto sãlė (m)	['sportɔ sa:'lʲe:]
tennis court	tèniso kòrtas (v)	['tʲɛnʲɪsɔ 'kortas]
garage	garãžas (v)	[ga'ra:ʒas]
private property	asmeninė nuosavýbė (m)	[asmɛ'nʲɪnʲe: nʊɑsa'vʲi:bʲe:]
warning sign	įspéjantis užrašas (v)	[i:s'pʲe:jantʲɪs 'ʊʒraʃas]

| security | apsaugà (m) | [apsɑu'ga] |
| security guard | apsauginis (v) | [apsɑu'gʲɪnʲɪs] |

renovations	remòntas (v)	[rʲɛ'montas]
to renovate (vt)	darýti remòntą	[da'rʲiːtʲɪ rʲɛ'monta:]
to put in order	tvarkýti	[tvar'kʲiːtʲɪ]
to paint (~ a wall)	dažýti	[da'ʒʲiːtʲɪ]
wallpaper	tapètai (v)	[ta'pʲɛtʌɪ]
to varnish (vt)	lakúoti	[lʲa'kʋɑtʲɪ]

pipe	vamzdis (v)	['vamzdʲɪs]
tools	įrankiai (v dgs)	['iːraŋkʲɛɪ]
basement	rūsỹs (v)	[ruː'sʲiːs]
sewerage (system)	kanalizãcija (m)	[kanalʲɪ'zaːtsʲɪjɛ]

14. House. Apartment. Part 2

apartment	bùtas (v)	['butas]
room	kambarỹs (v)	[kamba'rʲiːs]
bedroom	miegamàsis (v)	[mʲiɛga'masʲɪs]
dining room	valgomàsis (v)	[valʲgo'masʲɪs]

living room	svečių̃ kambarỹs (v)	[svʲɛ'tʂʲu: kamba'rʲiːs]
study (home office)	kabinètas (v)	[kabʲɪ'nʲɛtas]
entry room	príeškambaris (v)	['prʲiɛʃkambarʲɪs]
bathroom (room with a bath or shower)	voniõs kambarỹs (v)	[vo'nʲoːs kamba'rʲiːs]

| half bath | tualètas (v) | [tʋa'lʲɛtas] |

| floor | griñdys (m dgs) | ['grʲɪndʲiːs] |
| ceiling | lùbos (m dgs) | ['lʲubos] |

to dust (vt)	valýti dùlkes	[va'lʲiːtʲɪ 'dulʲkʲɛs]
vacuum cleaner	dulkių siurblỹs (v)	['dulʲkʲu: sʲʋr'blʲiːs]
to vacuum (vt)	siurbti	['sʲʋrptʲɪ]

mop	plaušinė šlúota (m)	[plʲɑu'ʃɪnʲe: 'ʃlʲʋɑta]
dust cloth	skùduras (v)	['skʋduras]
short broom	šlúota (m)	['ʃlʲʋɑta]
dustpan	semtuvėlis (v)	[sʲɛmtʋvʲeːlʲɪs]

furniture	baldai (v)	['balʲdʌɪ]
table	stãlas (v)	['staːlʲas]
chair	kėdė̃ (m)	[kʲeː'dʲeː]
armchair	fòtelis (v)	['fotʲɛlʲɪs]

bookcase	spìnta (m)	['spʲɪnta]
shelf	lentýna (m)	[lʲɛn'tʲiːna]
wardrobe	drabùžių spìnta (m)	[dra'bʋʒʲu: 'spʲɪnta]
mirror	véidrodis (v)	['vʲɛɪdrodʲɪs]

carpet	kìlimas (v)	['kʲɪlʲɪmas]
fireplace	židinỹs (v)	[ʒʲɪdʲɪ'nʲiːs]
drapes	užúolaidos (m dgs)	[ʊ'ʒʊalʲʌɪdos]
table lamp	stalìnė lémpa (m)	[sta'lʲɪnʲe: 'lʲempa]
chandelier	sietýnas (v)	[sʲie'tʲiːnas]

kitchen	virtùvė (m)	[vʲɪr'tʊvʲe:]
gas stove (range)	dùjinė (m)	['dʊjinʲe:]
electric stove	elektrìnė (m)	[ɛlʲɛk'trʲɪnʲe:]
microwave oven	mikrobangų krosnėlė (m)	[mʲɪkroban'gu: kros'nʲælʲe:]

refrigerator	šaldytùvas (v)	[ʃalʲdʲiː'tʊvas]
freezer	šáldymo kãmera (m)	['ʃalʲdʲiːmɔ 'ka:mʲɛra]
dishwasher	iñdų plovìmo mašinà (m)	['ɪndu: plʲo'vʲɪmɔ maʃɪ'na]
faucet	čiáupas (v)	['tʂʲæʊpas]

meat grinder	mėsmalė (m)	['mʲe:smalʲe:]
juicer	sulčiãspaudė (m)	[sʊlʲ'tʂʲæspaʊdʲe:]
toaster	tòsteris (v)	['tostʲɛrʲɪs]
mixer	mìkseris (v)	['mʲɪksʲɛrʲɪs]

coffee machine	kavõs aparãtas (v)	[ka'voːs apa'ra:tas]
kettle	arbatinùkas (v)	[arbatʲɪ'nʊkas]
teapot	arbãtinis (v)	[arba:'tʲɪnʲɪs]

TV set	televìzorius (v)	[tʲɛlʲɛ'vʲɪzorʲʊs]
VCR (video recorder)	video magnetofõnas (v)	[vʲɪdʲɛɔ magnʲɛto'fonas]
iron (e.g., steam ~)	lygintùvas (v)	[lʲiːgʲɪn'tʊvas]
telephone	telefònas (v)	[tʲɛlʲɛ'fonas]

15. Professions. Social status

director	direktorius (v)	[dʲɪ'rʲɛktorʲʊs]
superior	vìršininkas (v)	['vʲɪrʃɪnʲɪŋkas]
president	prezideñtas (v)	[prʲɛzʲɪ'dʲɛntas]
assistant	padėjėjas (v)	[padʲe:'je:jas]
secretary	sekretõrius (v)	[sʲɛkrʲɛ'to:rʲʊs]

owner, proprietor	valdýtojas (v)	[valʲ'dʲiːto:jɛs]
partner	pártneris (v)	['partnʲɛrʲɪs]
stockholder	ãkcininkas (v)	['a:ktsʲɪnʲɪŋkas]

businessman	komersántas (v)	[komʲɛr'santas]
millionaire	milijoniẽrius (v)	[mʲɪlʲɪjo'nʲɛrʲʊs]
billionaire	milijardiẽrius (v)	[mʲɪlʲɪjar'dʲɛrʲʊs]

actor	ãktorius (v)	['a:ktorʲʊs]
architect	architèktas (v)	[arxʲɪ'tʲɛktas]
banker	bánkininkas (v)	['baŋkʲɪnʲɪŋkas]
broker	bròkeris (v)	['brokʲɛrʲɪs]

veterinarian	veterinãras (v)	[vʲɛtʲɛrʲɪ'na:ras]
doctor	gýdytojas (v)	['gʲiːdʲiːto:jɛs]
chambermaid	kambarìnė (m)	[kamba'rʲɪnʲe:]
designer	dizáineris (v)	[dʲɪ'zʌɪnʲɛrʲɪs]
correspondent	korespondeñtas (v)	[korɛspon'dʲɛntas]
delivery man	kùrjeris (v)	['kurjɛrʲɪs]

electrician	mònteris (v)	['montʲɛrʲɪs]
musician	muzikántas (v)	[muzʲɪ'kantas]
babysitter	áuklė (m)	['ɑuklʲe:]
hairdresser	kirpėjas (v)	[kʲɪr'pʲe:jas]
herder, shepherd	piemuõ (v)	[pʲiɛ'muɑ]

singer (masc.)	daininiñkas (v)	[dʌɪnʲɪ'nʲɪŋkas]
translator	vertėjas (v)	[vʲɛr'tʲe:jas]
writer	rašýtojas (v)	[ra'ʃɪ:to:jɛs]
carpenter	dailìdė (v)	[dʌɪ'lʲɪdʲe:]
cook	virėjas (v)	[vʲɪ'rʲe:jas]

fireman	gaĩsrininkas (v)	['gʌɪsrʲɪnʲɪŋkas]
police officer	polìcininkas (v)	[po'lʲɪtsʲɪnʲɪŋkas]
mailman	pãštininkas (v)	['pa:ʃtʲɪnʲɪŋkas]
programmer	programúotojas (v)	[progra'muɑto:jɛs]
salesman (store staff)	pardavėjas (v)	[parda'vʲe:jas]

worker	darbiniñkas (v)	[darbʲɪ'nʲɪŋkas]
gardener	sõdininkas (v)	['so:dʲɪnʲɪŋkas]
plumber	santèchnikas (v)	[san'tʲɛxnʲɪkas]
dentist	stomatològas (v)	[stomato'lʲogas]
flight attendant (fem.)	stiuardèsė (m)	[stʲuar'dʲɛsʲe:]

dancer (masc.)	šokėjas (v)	[ʃo'kʲe:jas]
bodyguard	asmeñs sargýbinis (v)	[as'mʲɛns sar'gʲiːbʲɪnʲɪs]
scientist	mókslininkas (v)	['mokslʲɪnʲɪŋkas]
schoolteacher	mókytojas (v)	['mokʲiːto:jɛs]

farmer	fèrmeris (v)	['fʲɛrmʲɛrʲɪs]
surgeon	chirùrgas (v)	[xʲɪ'rurgas]
miner	šãchtininkas (v)	['ʃa:xtʲɪnʲɪŋkas]
chef (kitchen chef)	vyriáusiasis virėjas (v)	[vʲiː'rʲæuʲsæsʲɪs vʲɪ'rʲe:jas]
driver	vairúotojas (v)	[vʌɪ'ruɑto:jɛs]

16. Sport

kind of sports	spòrto šakà (m)	['sportɔ ʃa'ka]
soccer	fùtbolas (v)	['futbolʲas]
hockey	lẽdo ritulỹs (v)	['lʲædɔ rʲɪtu'lʲiː:s]
basketball	krepšìnis (v)	[krʲɛp'ʃɪnʲɪs]
baseball	beĩsbolas (v)	['bʲɛɪsbolʲas]
volleyball	tinklìnis (v)	[tʲɪŋk'lʲɪnʲɪs]

boxing	bòksas (v)	['boksas]
wrestling	imtỹnės (m dgs)	[ɪmˈtʲiːnʲeːs]
tennis	tènisas (v)	[ˈtʲɛnʲɪsas]
swimming	plaukìmas (v)	[plʲɑʊˈkʲɪmas]

chess	šachmãtai (v dgs)	[ʃaxˈmaːtʌɪ]
running	bėgìmas (v)	[bʲeːˈgʲɪmas]
athletics	lengvóji atlètika (m)	[lʲɛngˈvoːjɪ atˈlʲɛtʲɪka]
figure skating	dailùsis čiuožìmas (v)	[dʌɪˈlʲʊsʲɪs tʃʲʊoˈʒʲɪmas]
cycling	dvìračių spòrtas (v)	['dvʲɪratʃʲʊ 'sportas]

billiards	biliárdas (v)	[bʲɪlʲɪˈjardas]
bodybuilding	kultūrìzmas (v)	[kʊlʲtuːˈrʲɪzmas]
golf	gòlfas (v)	['golʲfas]
scuba diving	nárdymas (v)	['nardʲiːmas]
sailing	buriãvimas (v)	[bʊˈrʲævʲɪmas]
archery	šáudymas ìš lañko (v)	['ʃɑʊdʲiːmas ɪʃ 'lʲaŋkɔ]

period, half	kėlinỹs (v)	[kʲeːlʲɪˈnʲiːs]
half-time	pértrauka (m)	['pʲɛrtrɑʊka]
tie	lýgiosios (m dgs)	['lʲiːgʲosʲos]
to tie (vi)	sužaìsti lygiomìs	[sʊˈʒʌɪstʲɪ lʲiːgʲoˈmʲɪs]

treadmill	bėgìmo takẽlis (v)	[bʲeːˈgʲɪmɔ taˈkʲælʲɪs]
player	žaidė́jas (v)	[ʒʌɪˈdʲeːjas]
substitute	atsargìnis žaidė́jas (v)	[atsarˈgʲɪnʲɪs ʒʌɪˈdʲeːjas]
substitutes bench	atsargìnių súolas (v)	[atsarˈgʲɪnʲuː 'sʊolʲas]
match	rungtỹnės (m dgs)	[rʊŋkˈtʲiːnʲeːs]
goal	vartai (v)	['vartʌɪ]
goalkeeper	vártininkas (v)	['vartʲɪnʲɪŋkas]
goal (score)	įvartis (v)	['iːvartʲɪs]

Olympic Games	Olìmpinės žaidỹnės (m dgs)	[oˈlʲɪmpʲɪnʲeːs ʒʌɪˈdʲiːnʲeːs]
to set a record	pasíekti rekòrdą	[paˈsʲiɛktʲɪ rʲɛˈkorda:]
final	finãlas (v)	[fʲɪˈnaːlʲas]
champion	čempiònas (v)	[tʃʲɛmˈpʲɪjonas]
championship	čempionãtas (v)	[tʃʲɛmpʲɪjoˈnaːtas]

winner	nugalė́tojas (v)	[nʊgaˈlʲeːtoːjɛs]
victory	pérgalė (m)	['pʲɛrgalʲeː]
to win (vi)	laimė́ti	[lʲʌɪˈmʲeːtʲɪ]
to lose (not win)	pralaimė́ti	[pralʲʌɪˈmʲeːtʲɪ]
medal	medãlis (v)	[mʲɛˈdaːlʲɪs]

first place	pirmóji vietà (m)	[pʲɪrˈmoːjɪ vʲɪɛˈta]
second place	antróji vietà (m)	[anˈtroːjɪ vʲɪɛˈta]
third place	trečióji vietà (m)	[trʲɛˈtʃʲoːjɪ vʲɪɛˈta]

stadium	stadiònas (v)	[stadʲɪˈonas]
fan, supporter	sirgãlius (v)	[sʲɪrˈgaːlʲʊs]
trainer, coach	trèneris (v)	['trʲɛnʲɛrʲɪs]
training	treniruõtė (m)	[trʲɛnʲɪˈrʊɑtʲeː]

95

17. Foreign languages. Orthography

language	kalbà (m)	[kalʲ"ba]
to study (vt)	studijúoti	[stʊdʲɪ'jʊatʲɪ]
pronunciation	tarìmas (v)	[ta'rʲɪmas]
accent	akceñtas (v)	[ak'tsʲɛntas]
noun	daiktãvardis (v)	[dʌɪk'ta:vardʲɪs]
adjective	bũdvardis (v)	['bu:dvardʲɪs]
verb	veiksmãžodis (v)	[vʲɛɪks'ma:ʒodʲɪs]
adverb	príeveiksmis (v)	['prʲɪɛvʲɛɪksmʲɪs]
pronoun	įvardis (v)	['i:vardʲɪs]
interjection	jaustùkas (v)	[jɛʊs'tʊkas]
preposition	príelinksnis (v)	['prʲɪɛlʲɪŋksnʲɪs]
root	žõdžio šaknìs (m)	['ʒo:dʒʲo ʃak'nʲɪs]
ending	galũnė (m)	[ga'lʲu:nʲe:]
prefix	príešdėlis (v)	['prʲɪɛʃdʲe:lʲɪs]
syllable	skiemuõ (v)	[skʲɪɛ'mʊa]
suffix	príesaga (m)	['prʲɪɛsaga]
stress mark	kìrtis (m)	['kʲɪrtʲɪs]
period, dot	tãškas (v)	['ta:ʃkas]
comma	kablēlis (v)	[kab'lʲælʲɪs]
colon	dvìtaškis (v)	['dvʲɪtaʃkʲɪs]
ellipsis	daũgtaškis (v)	['daʊktaʃkʲɪs]
question	kláusimas (v)	['klʲaʊsʲɪmas]
question mark	klaustùkas (v)	[klʲaʊ'stʊkas]
exclamation point	šauktùkas (v)	[ʃaʊk'tʊkas]
in quotation marks	kabùtėse	[ka'bʊtʲe:se]
in parenthesis	skliaustėliuose	[sklʲɛʊ'stʲælʲʊosʲɛ]
letter	raĩdė (m)	['rʌɪdʲe:]
capital letter	didžioji raĩdė (m)	[dʲɪ'dʒʲo:jɪ 'rʌɪdʲe:]
sentence	sakinỹs (v)	[sakʲɪ'nʲi:s]
group of words	žõdžių junginỹs (v)	['ʒo:dʒʲu: jungʲɪ'nʲi:s]
expression	išsireiškìmas (v)	[ɪʃsʲɪrʲɛɪʃ'kʲɪmas]
subject	veiksnỹs (v)	[vʲɛɪks'nʲi:s]
predicate	tarinỹs (v)	[tarʲɪ'nʲi:s]
line	eilùtė (m)	[ɛɪ'lʲʊtʲe:]
paragraph	pastraĩpa (m)	[past'rʌɪpa]
synonym	sinonìmas (v)	[sʲɪno'nʲɪmas]
antonym	antonìmas (v)	[anto'nʲɪmas]
exception	išimtìs (m)	[ɪʃʲɪm'tʲɪs]
to underline (vt)	pabraũkti	[pa'braʊktʲɪ]
rules	taisỹklės (m dgs)	[tʌɪ'sʲi:klʲe:s]

grammar	gramãtika (m)	[gra'ma:tʲɪka]
vocabulary	lẽksika (m)	['lʲɛksʲɪka]
phonetics	fonẽtika (m)	[fo'nʲɛtʲɪka]
alphabet	abẽcẽlẽ (m)	[abʲe:'tsʲe:lʲe:]

textbook	vadovẽlis (v)	[vado'vʲe:lʲɪs]
dictionary	žodýnas (v)	[ʒo'dʲi:nas]
phrasebook	pasikalbẽjimų knygẽlẽ (m)	[pasʲɪkalʲʲbʲɛjɪmu: knʲi:'gʲælʲe:]

word	žõdis (v)	['ʒo:dʲɪs]
meaning	prasmẽ (m)	[pras'mʲe:]
memory	atmintìs (m)	[atmʲɪn'tʲɪs]

18. The Earth. Geography

the Earth	Žẽmẽ (m)	['ʒʲæmʲe:]
the globe (the Earth)	žẽmẽs rutulýs (v)	['ʒʲæmʲe:s rutu'lʲi:s]
planet	planetà (m)	[plʲanʲɛ'ta]

geography	geogrãfija (m)	[gʲɛo'gra:fʲɪjɛ]
nature	gamtà (m)	[gam'ta]
map	žemẽlapis (v)	[ʒe'mʲe:lʲapʲɪs]
atlas	ãtlasas (v)	['a:tlʲasas]

in the north	šiáurẽje	['ʃæurʲe:je]
in the south	pietuosè	[pʲɪɛtua'sʲɛ]
in the west	vakaruosè	[vakarua'sʲɛ]
in the east	rytuosè	[rʲi:tua'sʲɛ]

sea	jũra (m)	['ju:ra]
ocean	vandenýnas (v)	[vandʲɛ'nʲi:nas]
gulf (bay)	įlanka (m)	['i:lʲaŋka]
straits	sąsiauris (v)	['sa:sʲɛurʲɪs]

continent (mainland)	žemýnas (v)	[ʒʲɛ'mʲi:nas]
island	salà (m)	[sa'lʲa]
peninsula	pusiãsalis (v)	[pu'sʲæsalʲɪs]
archipelago	archipelãgas (v)	[arxʲɪpʲɛ'lʲa:gas]

harbor	úostas (v)	['uastas]
coral reef	korãlų rìfas (v)	[ko'ra:lʲu: 'rʲɪfas]
shore	pajũris (v)	['pajūrʲɪs]
coast	pakrántẽ (m)	[pak'rantʲe:]

| flow (flood tide) | antplũdis (v) | ['antplʲu:dʲɪs] |
| ebb (ebb tide) | atóslũgis (v) | [a'toslʲu:gʲɪs] |

| latitude | platumà (m) | [plʲatu'ma] |
| longitude | ilgumà (m) | [ɪlʲgu'ma] |

| parallel | paralelė (m) | [para'lʲɛlʲeː] |
| equator | ekvātorius (v) | [ɛk'va:torʲus] |

sky	dangùs (v)	[dan'gʊs]
horizon	horizòntas (v)	[ɣorʲɪ'zontas]
atmosphere	atmosferà (m)	[atmosfʲɛ'ra]

mountain	kálnas (v)	['kalʲnas]
summit, top	viršū́nė (m)	[vʲɪrʲʃuːnʲeː]
cliff	uolà (m)	[ʊa'lʲla]
hill	kalvà (m)	[kalʲ'va]

volcano	ugnìkalnis (v)	[ʊg'nʲɪkalʲnʲɪs]
glacier	ledýnas (v)	[lʲɛ'dʲi:nas]
waterfall	krioklỹs (v)	[krʲok'lʲi:s]
plain	lygumà (m)	[lʲi:gʊ'ma]

river	ùpė (m)	['ʊpʲeː]
spring (natural source)	šaltìnis (v)	[ʃalʲ'tʲɪnʲɪs]
bank (of river)	kraňtas (v)	['krantas]
downstream (adv)	pasroviuì	[pasro'vʲʊɪ]
upstream (adv)	priẽš srõvę	['prʲɛʃ 'sro:vʲɛ]

lake	ẽžeras (v)	['ɛʒʲɛras]
dam	ùžtvanka (m)	['ʊʒtvaŋka]
canal	kanãlas (v)	[ka'na:lʲas]
swamp (marshland)	pélkė (m)	['pʲɛlʲkʲeː]
ice	lẽdas (v)	['lʲædas]

19. Countries of the world. Part 1

Europe	Europà (m)	[ɛʊro'pa]
European Union	europiẽtis (v)	[ɛʊro'pʲɛtʲɪs]
European (n)	europiẽtė (m)	[ɛʊro'pʲɛtʲeː]
European (adj)	europiẽtiškas	[ɛʊro'pʲɛtʲɪʃkas]

Austria	Áustrija (m)	['ɑʊstrʲɪjɛ]
Great Britain	Didžióji Britãnija (m)	[dʲɪ'dʒʲo:jɪ brʲɪ'ta:nʲɪjɛ]
England	Ánglija (m)	['anglʲɪjɛ]
Belgium	Bèlgija (m)	['bʲɛlʲgʲɪjɛ]
Germany	Vokietìja (m)	[vokʲiɛ'tʲɪja]

Netherlands	Nýderlandai (v dgs)	['nʲi:dʲɛrlʲandʌɪ]
Holland	Olándija (m)	[o'lʲandʲɪjɛ]
Greece	Graĩkija (m)	['grʌɪkʲɪjɛ]
Denmark	Dãnija (m)	['da:nʲɪjɛ]
Ireland	Aĩrija (m)	['ʌɪrʲɪjɛ]

| Iceland | Islándija (m) | [ɪs'lʲandʲɪjɛ] |
| Spain | Ispãnija (m) | [ɪs'pa:nʲɪjɛ] |

Italy	Itālija (m)	[ɪ'ta:lʲɪjɛ]
Cyprus	Kìpras (v)	['kʲɪpras]
Malta	Màlta (m)	['malʲta]

Norway	Norvègija (m)	[nor'vʲɛɡʲɪjɛ]
Portugal	Portugālija (m)	[portʊ'ga:lʲɪjɛ]
Finland	Súomija (m)	['sʊɑmʲɪjɛ]
France	Prancūzijà (m)	[prantsu:zʲɪ'ja]
Sweden	Švèdija (m)	['ʃvʲɛdʲɪjɛ]

Switzerland	Šveicārija (m)	[ʃvʲɛɪ'tsa:rʲɪjɛ]
Scotland	Škòtija (m)	['ʃkotʲɪjɛ]
Vatican	Vatikānas (v)	[vatʲɪka:nas]
Liechtenstein	Lìchtenšteinas (v)	['lʲɪxtʲɛnʃtʲɛɪnas]
Luxembourg	Liùksemburgas (v)	['lʲʊksʲɛmbʊrgas]

Monaco	Mònakas (v)	['monakas]
Albania	Albānija (m)	[alʲ'ba:nʲɪjɛ]
Bulgaria	Bulgārija (m)	[bʊlʲ'ga:rʲɪjɛ]
Hungary	Veñgrija (m)	['vʲɛŋgrʲɪjɛ]
Latvia	Lãtvija (m)	['lʲa:tvʲɪjɛ]

Lithuania	Lietuvà (m)	[lʲiɛtʊ'va]
Poland	Lénkija (m)	['lʲɛŋkʲɪjɛ]
Romania	Rumùnija (m)	[rʊ'mʊnʲɪjɛ]
Serbia	Sèrbija (m)	['sʲɛrbʲɪjɛ]
Slovakia	Slovãkija (m)	[slʲo'va:kʲɪjɛ]

Croatia	Kroãtija (m)	[kro'a:tʲɪjɛ]
Czech Republic	Čèkija (m)	['tʂʲɛkʲɪjɛ]
Estonia	Èstija (m)	['ɛstʲɪjɛ]
Bosnia and Herzegovina	Bòsnija ìr Hercegovinà (m)	['bosnʲɪja ir ɣʲɛrtsʲɛgovʲɪ'na]
Macedonia (Republic of ~)	Makedònija (m)	[makʲɛ'donʲɪjɛ]

Slovenia	Slovénija (m)	[slʲo'vʲe:nʲɪjɛ]
Montenegro	Juodkalnijà (m)	[jʊɑdkalʲnʲɪ'ja]
Belarus	Baltarùsija (m)	[balʲta'rʊsʲɪjɛ]
Moldova, Moldavia	Moldāvija (m)	[molʲ'da:vʲɪjɛ]
Russia	Rùsija (m)	['rʊsʲɪjɛ]
Ukraine	Ukrainà (m)	[ʊkrʌɪ'na]

20. Countries of the world. Part 2

Asia	āzija (m)	['a:zʲɪjɛ]
Vietnam	Vietnāmas (v)	[vʲɛt'na:mas]
India	Ìndija (m)	['ɪndʲɪjɛ]
Israel	Izraèlis (v)	[ɪzraʲɛlʲɪs]
China	Kìnija (m)	['kʲɪnʲɪjɛ]
Lebanon	Libānas (v)	[lʲɪ'banas]

Mongolia	Mongòlija (m)	[mon'gol'ɪjɛ]
Malaysia	Malàizija (m)	[ma'l'ʌɪz'ɪjɛ]
Pakistan	Pakistãnas (v)	[pak'ɪ'sta:nas]
Saudi Arabia	Saùdo Arãbija (m)	[sa'ʊdɔ a'ra:b'ɪjɛ]

Thailand	Tailàndas (v)	[tʌɪ'l'andas]
Taiwan	Taivãnis (v)	[tʌɪ'van'ɪs]
Turkey	Tur̃kija (m)	['tʊrk'ɪjɛ]
Japan	Japònija (m)	[ja'pon'ɪjɛ]
Afghanistan	Afganistãnas (v)	[afgan'ɪ'sta:nas]

Bangladesh	Bangladèšas (v)	[bangl'a'd'ɛʃas]
Indonesia	Indonezijà (m)	[ɪndon'ɛz'ɪ'ja]
Jordan	Jordãnija (m)	[jɔr'da:n'ɪjɛ]
Iraq	Irãkas (v)	[ɪ'ra:kas]
Iran	Irãnas (v)	[ɪ'ra:nas]

Cambodia	Kambodžà (m)	[kambo'dʒa]
Kuwait	Kuveìtas (v)	[kʊ'v'ɛɪtas]
Laos	Laòsas (v)	[l'a'osas]
Myanmar	Mianmãras (v)	[m'æn'ma:ras]
Nepal	Nepãlas (v)	[n'ɛ'pa:l'as]

United Arab Emirates	Jungtìniai Arãbų Emiratai (v dgs)	[jʊŋk't'ɪn'ɛɪ a'ra:bu: ɛm'ɪratʌɪ]
Syria	Sìrija (m)	['s'ɪr'ɪjɛ]
Palestine	Palestìna (m)	[pal'ɛs't'ɪna]
South Korea	Pietŭ̃ Koréja (m)	[p'ɪɛ'tu: ko'r'e:ja]
North Korea	Šiáurės Koréja (m)	['ʃæʊr'e:s ko'r'e:ja]

United States of America	Jungtìnės Amèrikos Valstìjos (m dgs)	[jʊŋk't'ɪn'e:s a'm'ɛr'ɪkos val's't'ɪjɔs]
Canada	Kanadà (m)	[kana'da]
Mexico	Mèksika (m)	['m'ɛks'ɪka]
Argentina	Argentinà (m)	[arg'ɛnt'ɪ'na]
Brazil	Brazìlija (m)	[bra'z'ɪl'ɪjɛ]

Colombia	Kolùmbija (m)	[kɔ'l'ʊmb'ɪjɛ]
Cuba	Kubà (m)	[kʊ'ba]
Chile	Čìlė (m)	['tʂ'ɪl'e:]
Venezuela	Venesuelà (m)	[v'ɛn'ɛsʊ'ɛ'l'a]
Ecuador	Ekvadòras (v)	[ɛkva'doras]

The Bahamas	Bahãmų salõs (m dgs)	[ba'ɣamu: 'sal'o:s]
Panama	Panamà (m)	[pana'ma]
Egypt	Egìptas (v)	[ɛ'g'ɪptas]
Morocco	Maròkas (v)	[ma'rokas]
Tunisia	Tunìsas (v)	[tʊ'n'ɪsas]
Kenya	Kènija (m)	['k'ɛn'ɪjɛ]
Libya	Lìbija (m)	['l'ɪb'ɪjɛ]
South Africa	Pietŭ̃ ãfrikos respùblika (m)	[p'ɪɛ'tu: 'a:fr'ɪkos r'ɛs'pʊbl'ɪka]

| Australia | Austrālija (m) | [ɑʊsˈtraːlʲɪjɛ] |
| New Zealand | Naujóji Zelándija (m) | [nɑʊˈjɔːjɪ zʲɛˈlʲandʲɪjɛ] |

21. Weather. Natural disasters

weather	óras (v)	[ˈoras]
weather forecast	óro prognózė (m)	[ˈorɔ progˈnozʲeː]
temperature	temperatūrà (m)	[tʲɛmpʲɛratuːˈra]
thermometer	termomètras (v)	[tʲɛrmoˈmʲɛtras]
barometer	barometras (v)	[baroˈmʲɛtras]

sun	sáulė (m)	[ˈsɑʊlʲeː]
to shine (vi)	šviẽsti	[ˈʃvʲɛstʲɪ]
sunny (day)	saulėta	[sɑʊˈlʲeːta]
to come up (vi)	pakìlti	[paˈkʲɪlʲtʲɪ]
to set (vi)	leĩstis	[ˈlʲɛɪstʲɪs]

rain	lietùs (v)	[lʲɛˈtʊs]
it's raining	lỹja	[ˈlʲiːja]
pouring rain	liūtis (m)	[ˈlʲuːtʲɪs]
rain cloud	debesìs (v)	[dʲɛbʲɛˈsʲɪs]
puddle	balà (m)	[baˈlʲa]
to get wet (in rain)	šlãpti	[ˈʃlʲaptʲɪ]

thunderstorm	perkūnija (m)	[pʲɛrˈkuːnʲɪjɛ]
lightning (~ strike)	žaĩbas (v)	[ˈʒʌɪbas]
to flash (vi)	žaibúoti	[ʒʌɪˈbʊɑtʲɪ]
thunder	griaustìnis (v)	[grʲɛʊsˈtʲɪnʲɪs]
it's thundering	griáudėja griaustìnis	[ˈgrʲæʊdʲɛːja grʲɛʊsˈtʲɪnʲɪs]
hail	krušà (m)	[krʊˈʃa]
it's hailing	kriñta krušà	[ˈkrʲɪnta krʊˈʃa]

heat (extreme ~)	kar̃štis (v)	[ˈkarʃtʲɪs]
it's hot	kar̃šta	[ˈkarʃta]
it's warm	šìlta	[ˈʃɪlʲta]
it's cold	šálta	[ˈʃalʲta]

fog (mist)	rūkas (v)	[ˈruːkas]
foggy	miglótas	[mʲɪgˈlʲotas]
cloud	debesìs (v)	[dʲɛbʲɛˈsʲɪs]
cloudy (adj)	debesúota	[dʲɛbʲɛˈsʊɑta]
humidity	drėgmė̃ (m)	[drʲeːgˈmʲeː]

snow	sniẽgas (v)	[ˈsnʲɛgas]
it's snowing	sniñga	[ˈsnʲɪnga]
frost (severe ~, freezing cold)	šáltis (v)	[ˈʃalʲtʲɪs]
below zero (adv)	žemiaũ nùlio	[ʒʲɛˈmʲɛʊ ˈnʊlʲɔ]
hoarfrost	šerkšnà (m)	[ʃʲɛrkʃˈna]
bad weather	dárgana (m)	[ˈdargana]

disaster	katastrofà (m)	[katastro'fa]
flood, inundation	pótvynis (v)	['potvʲiːnʲɪs]
avalanche	lavinà (m)	[lʲavʲɪ'na]
earthquake	žẽmės drebéjimas (v)	['ʒʲæmʲeːs dre'bʲɛjɪmas]

tremor, quake	smũgis (m)	['smuːgʲɪs]
epicenter	epiceñtras (v)	[ɛpʲɪ'tsʲɛntras]
eruption	iššiveržìmas (v)	[ɪʃʲʃʲɪvʲɛr'ʒʲɪmas]
lava	lavà (m)	[lʲa'va]

tornado	tornãdo (v)	[tor'naːdɔ]
twister	víesulas (v)	['vʲiɛsulʲas]
hurricane	uragãnas (v)	[ura'gaːnas]
tsunami	cunãmis (v)	[tsu'naːmʲɪs]
cyclone	ciklònas (v)	[tsʲɪk'lʲonas]

22. Animals. Part 1

| animal | gyvũnas (v) | [gʲiː'vuːnas] |
| predator | plėšrũnas (v) | [plʲeʃru:nas] |

tiger	tìgras (v)	['tʲɪgras]
lion	liũtas (v)	['lʲuːtas]
wolf	vìlkas (v)	['vʲɪlʲkas]
fox	lãpė (m)	['lʲaːpʲeː]
jaguar	jaguãras (v)	[jagu'aːras]

lynx	lũšis (m)	['lʲuːʃɪs]
coyote	kojòtas (v)	[kɔ'jɔ tas]
jackal	šakãlas (v)	[ʃa'kaːlʲas]
hyena	hienà (m)	[xʲiɛ'na]

squirrel	voverẽ (m)	[vove'rʲeː]
hedgehog	ežỹs (v)	[ɛʒʲiːs]
rabbit	triùšis (v)	['trʲuʃɪs]
raccoon	meškénas (v)	[mʲɛʃʲkʲeːnas]

hamster	žiurkénas (v)	[ʒʲur'kʲeːnas]
mole	kùrmis (v)	['kurmʲɪs]
mouse	pelẽ (m)	[pʲɛ'lʲeː]
rat	žiùrkė (m)	['ʒʲurkʲeː]
bat	šikšnósparnis (v)	[ʃɪkʃ'nospɑrnʲɪs]

beaver	bẽbras (v)	['bʲæbras]
horse	arklỹs (v)	[ark'lʲiːs]
deer	élnias (v)	['ɛlʲnʲæs]
camel	kupranugãris (v)	[kupranu'gaːrʲɪs]
zebra	zèbras (v)	['zʲɛbras]
whale	bangìnis (v)	[ban'gʲɪnʲɪs]
seal	rúonis (v)	['ruɑnʲɪs]

| walrus | vėplỹs (v) | [vʲeːpʲlʲiːs] |
| dolphin | delfinas (v) | [dʲɛlʲˈfʲɪnas] |

bear	lokỹs (v), meška (m)	[lʲoˈkʲiːs], [mʲɛʃˈka]
monkey	beždžiõnė (m)	[bʲɛʒʹdʒʲoːnʲeː]
elephant	dramblỹs (v)	[dramˈbʲlʲiːs]
rhinoceros	raganõsis (v)	[ragaˈnoːsʲɪs]
giraffe	žirafà (m)	[ʒʲɪraˈfa]

hippopotamus	begemõtas (v)	[bʲɛgʲɛˈmotas]
kangaroo	kengūrà (m)	[kʲɛnˈguːˈra]
cat	katė̃ (m)	[kaˈtʲeː]
dog	šuõ (v)	[ˈʃʊɑ]

cow	kárvė (m)	[ˈkarvʲeː]
bull	bùlius (v)	[ˈbʊlʲʊs]
sheep (ewe)	avìs (m)	[aˈvʲɪs]
goat	ožkà (m)	[oʒˈka]

donkey	ãsilas (v)	[ˈaːsʲɪlʲas]
pig, hog	kiaũlė (m)	[ˈkʲɛʊlʲeː]
hen (chicken)	vištà (m)	[vʲɪʃˈta]
rooster	gaidỹs (v)	[gʌɪˈdʲiːs]

duck	ántis (m)	[ˈantʲɪs]
goose	žą̃sinas (v)	[ˈʒaːsʲɪnas]
turkey (hen)	kalakùtė (m)	[kalʲaˈkʊtʲeː]
sheepdog	avìganis (v)	[aˈvʲɪganʲɪs]

23. Animals. Part 2

bird	paũkštis (v)	[ˈpɑʊkʃtʲɪs]
pigeon	balañdis (v)	[baˈlʲanʲdʲɪs]
sparrow	žvìrblis (v)	[ˈʒvʲɪrbʲlʲɪs]
tit (great tit)	zýlė (m)	[ˈzʲiːlʲeː]
magpie	šárka (m)	[ˈʃarka]

eagle	erẽlis (v)	[ɛˈrʲælʲɪs]
hawk	vãnagas (v)	[ˈvaːnagas]
falcon	sãkalas (v)	[ˈsaːkalʲas]

swan	gulbė̃ (m)	[ˈgʊlʲbʲeː]
crane	gérvė (m)	[ˈgʲɛrvʲeː]
stork	gañdras (v)	[ˈgandras]
parrot	papūgà (m)	[papuˈʹga]
peacock	póvas (v)	[ˈpovas]
ostrich	strùtis (v)	[ˈstrʊtʲɪs]

| heron | garnỹs (v) | [garˈnʲiːs] |
| nightingale | lakštiñgala (m) | [lʲakʃˈtʲɪŋgalʲa] |

swallow	kregždė (m)	[krʲɛgʒˈdʲeː]
woodpecker	genỹs (v)	[gʲɛˈnʲiːs]
cuckoo	gegutė (m)	[gʲɛˈgutʲeː]
owl	peléda (m)	[pʲɛˈlʲeːda]

penguin	pingvìnas (v)	[pʲɪngˈvʲɪnas]
tuna	tùnas (v)	[ˈtunas]
trout	upétakis (v)	[ʊˈpʲeːtakʲɪs]
eel	ungurỹs (v)	[ʊnguˈrʲiːs]

shark	ryklỹs (v)	[rʲɪkˈlʲiːs]
crab	krãbas (v)	[ˈkraːbas]
jellyfish	medūzà (m)	[mʲɛduːˈza]
octopus	aštuonkõjis (v)	[aʃtʊɑŋˈkoːjis]

starfish	jū́ros žvaigždė̃ (m)	[ˈjuːros ʒvʌɪgʒˈdʲeː]
sea urchin	jū́ros ežỹs (v)	[ˈjuːros ɛˈʒʲiːs]
seahorse	jū́ros arkliùkas (v)	[ˈjuːros arkˈlʲʊkas]
shrimp	krevètė (m)	[krʲɛˈvʲɛtʲeː]

snake	gyvãtė (m)	[gʲiːˈvaːtʲeː]
viper	angìs (v)	[anˈgʲɪs]
lizard	dríežas (v)	[ˈdrʲiɛʒas]
iguana	iguanà (m)	[ɪgʊaˈna]
chameleon	chameleònas (v)	[xamʲɛlʲɛˈonas]
scorpion	skorpiònas (v)	[skorpʲɪˈɔnas]

turtle	vėžlỹs (v)	[vʲeːˈʒˈlʲiːs]
frog	varlė̃ (m)	[varˈlʲeː]
crocodile	krokodìlas (v)	[krokoˈdʲɪlʲas]

insect, bug	vabzdỹs (v)	[vabzˈdʲiːs]
butterfly	drugẽlis (v)	[drʊˈgʲælʲɪs]
ant	skruzdélė (m)	[skrʊzˈdʲælʲeː]
fly	mùsė (m)	[ˈmʊsʲeː]

mosquito	úodas (v)	[ˈʊɑdas]
beetle	vãbalas (v)	[ˈva:balʲas]
bee	bìtė (m)	[ˈbʲɪtʲeː]
spider	vóras (v)	[ˈvoras]

24. Trees. Plants

tree	mẽdis (v)	[ˈmʲædʲɪs]
birch	béržas (v)	[ˈbʲɛrʒas]
oak	ą́žuolas (v)	[ˈaːʒʊɑlʲas]
linden tree	líepa (m)	[ˈlʲiɛpa]
aspen	drebulė̃ (m)	[drebʊˈlʲeː]
maple	klẽvas (v)	[ˈklʲævas]
spruce	ẽglė (m)	[ˈʲæglʲeː]

| pine | pušis (m) | [pʊˈʃɪs] |
| cedar | kedras (v) | [ˈkʲɛdras] |

poplar	tuopa (m)	[ˈtʊɑpa]
rowan	šermukšnis (v)	[ʃʲɛrˈmʊkʃnʲɪs]
beech	bukas (v)	[ˈbʊkas]
elm	guoba (m)	[ˈgʊɑba]

ash (tree)	uosis (v)	[ˈʊɑsʲɪs]
chestnut	kaštonas (v)	[kaʃˈtoːnas]
palm tree	palmė (m)	[ˈpalʲmʲeː]
bush	krūmas (v)	[ˈkruːmas]

mushroom	grybas (v)	[ˈgrʲiːbas]
poisonous mushroom	nuodingas grybas (v)	[nʊɑˈdʲɪngas ˈgrʲiːbas]
cep (Boletus edulis)	baravykas (v)	[baraˈvʲiːkas]
russula	ūmėdė (m)	[uːmʲeːˈdʲeː]
fly agaric	musmirė (m)	[ˈmʊsmʲɪrʲeː]
death cap	šungrybis (v)	[ˈʃʊngrʲiːbʲɪs]

flower	gėlė (m)	[gʲeːˈlʲeː]
bouquet (of flowers)	puokštė (m)	[ˈpʊɑkʃtʲeː]
rose (flower)	rožė (m)	[ˈroːʒʲeː]
tulip	tulpė (m)	[ˈtʊlʲpʲeː]
carnation	gvazdikas (v)	[gvazˈdʲɪkas]

camomile	ramunė (m)	[raˈmʊnʲeː]
cactus	kaktusas (v)	[ˈkaːktʊsas]
lily of the valley	pakalnutė (m)	[pakalʲˈnʊtʲeː]
snowdrop	sniegena (m)	[ˈsnʲɛgʲɛna]
water lily	vandens lelija (m)	[vanˈdʲɛns lʲɛlʲɪˈja]

greenhouse (tropical ~)	oranžerija (m)	[oranˈʒʲɛrʲɪjɛ]
lawn	gazonas (v)	[gaˈzonas]
flowerbed	klomba (m)	[ˈklʲomba]

plant	augalas (v)	[ˈɑʊgalʲas]
grass	žolė (m)	[ʒoˈlʲeː]
leaf	lapas (v)	[ˈlʲaːpas]
petal	žiedlapis (v)	[ˈʒʲiɛdlʲapʲɪs]
stem	stiebas (v)	[ˈstʲiɛbas]
young plant (shoot)	želmuo (v)	[ʒʲɛlʲˈmʊɑ]

cereal crops	grūdinės kultūros (m dgs)	[gruːˈdʲɪnʲeːs kʊlʲˈtuːros]
wheat	kviečiai (v dgs)	[kvʲiɛˈtʂʲɛɪ]
rye	rugiai (v dgs)	[rʊˈgʲɛɪ]
oats	avižos (m dgs)	[ˈaːvʲɪʒos]

millet	sora (m)	[ˈsora]
barley	miežiai (v dgs)	[ˈmʲɛʒʲɛɪ]
corn	kukurūzas (v)	[kʊkʊˈruːzas]
rice	ryžiai (v)	[ˈrʲiːʒʲɛɪ]

25. Various useful words

balance (of situation)	balánsas (v)	[ba'lʲansas]
base (basis)	bãzė (m)	['ba:zʲe:]
beginning	pradžià (m)	[prad'ʒʲæ]
category	kategòrija (m)	[katʲɛ'gorʲɪjɛ]
choice	pasirinkìmas (v)	[pasʲɪrʲɪŋ'kʲɪmas]
coincidence	sutapìmas (v)	[suta'pʲɪmas]
comparison	palýginimas (v)	[pa'lʲi:gʲɪnʲɪmas]
degree (extent, amount)	láipsnis (v)	['lʲʌɪpsnʲɪs]
development	výstymas (v)	['vʲi:stʲi:mas]
difference	skìrtumas (v)	['skʲɪrtumas]
effect (e.g., of drugs)	efèktas (v)	[ɛ'fʲɛktas]
effort (exertion)	pãstangos (m dgs)	['pa:stangos]
element	elemeñtas (v)	[ɛlʲɛ'mʲɛntas]
example (illustration)	pavyzdỹs (v)	[pavʲi:z'dʲi:s]
fact	fãktas (v)	['fa:ktas]
help	pagálba (m)	[pa'galʲba]
ideal	ideãlas (v)	[idʲɛ'a:lʲas]
kind (sort, type)	rū̃šis (m)	['ru:ʃɪs]
mistake, error	klaidà (m)	[klʲʌɪ'da]
moment	momeñtas (v)	[mo'mʲɛntas]
obstacle	kliūtis (m)	['klʲu:tʲɪs]
part (~ of sth)	dalìs (m)	[da'lʲɪs]
pause (break)	páuzė (m)	['pɑuzʲe:]
position	pozìcija (m)	[po'zʲɪtsʲɪjɛ]
problem	problemà (m)	[problʲɛ'ma]
process	procèsas (v)	[pro'tsʲɛsas]
progress	progrèsas (v)	[pro'grʲɛsas]
property (quality)	savýbė (m)	[sa'vʲi:bʲe:]
reaction	reãkcija (m)	[rʲɛ'a:ktsʲɪjɛ]
risk	rìzika (m)	['rʲɪzʲɪka]
secret	paslaptìs (m)	[paslʲap'tʲɪs]
series	sèrija (m)	['sʲɛrʲɪjɛ]
shape (outer form)	fòrma (m)	['forma]
situation	situãcija (m)	[sʲɪ'tua:tsʲɪjɛ]
solution	sprendìmas (v)	[sprʲɛn'dʲɪmas]
standard (adj)	standártinis	[stan'dartʲɪnʲɪs]
stop (pause)	sustojìmas (v)	[susto'jɪmas]
style	stìlius (v)	['stʲɪlʲus]
system	sistemà (m)	[sʲɪstʲɛ'ma]

| table (chart) | lentelė (m) | [lʲɛn'tʲælʲe:] |
| tempo, rate | tempas (v) | ['tʲɛmpas] |

term (word, expression)	terminas (v)	['tʲɛrmʲɪnas]
truth (e.g., moment of ~)	tiesa (m)	[tʲɛ'sa]
turn (please wait your ~)	eilė (m)	[ɛɪ'lʲe:]
urgent (adj)	skubus	[skʊ'bʊs]

utility (usefulness)	nauda (m)	[nɑʊ'da]
variant (alternative)	variantas (v)	[varʲɪ'jantas]
way (means, method)	būdas (v)	['bu:das]
zone	zona (m)	[zo'na]

26. Modifiers. Adjectives. Part 1

additional (adj)	papildomas	[pa'pʲɪlʲdomas]
ancient (~ civilization)	senovinis	[sʲɛ'novʲɪnʲɪs]
artificial (adj)	dirbtinis	[dʲɪrp'tʲɪnʲɪs]
bad (adj)	blogas	['blʲo:gas]
beautiful (person)	gražus	[gra'ʒʊs]

big (in size)	didelis	['dʲɪdʲɛlʲɪs]
bitter (taste)	kartus	[kar'tʊs]
blind (sightless)	aklas	['a:klʲas]
central (adj)	centrinis	[tsʲɛn'trʲɪnʲɪs]

children's (adj)	vaikiškas	['vʌɪkʲɪʃkas]
clandestine (secret)	pogrindinis	['pogrʲɪndʲɪnʲɪs]
clean (free from dirt)	švarus	[ʃva'rʊs]
clever (smart)	protingas	[pro'tʲɪngas]
compatible (adj)	suderinamas	[sʊ'dʲærʲɪnamas]

contented (satisfied)	patenkintas	[pa'tʲɛŋkʲɪntas]
dangerous (adj)	pavojingas	[pavo'jɪngas]
dead (not alive)	miręs	['mʲɪrʲɛ:s]
dense (fog, smoke)	tirštas	['tʲɪrʃtas]
difficult (decision)	sunkus	[sʊŋ'kʊs]

dirty (not clean)	purvinas	['pʊrvʲɪnas]
easy (not difficult)	paprastas	['paprastas]
empty (glass, room)	tuščias	['tʊʃʦʲæs]
exact (amount)	tikslus	[tʲɪks'lʲʊs]
excellent (adj)	puikus	[pʊi'kʊs]

excessive (adj)	besaikis	[bʲɛ'sʌɪkʲɪs]
exterior (adj)	išorinis	[ɪʃo'rʲɪnʲɪs]
fast (quick)	greitas	['grʲɛɪtas]
fertile (land, soil)	vaisingas	[vʌɪ'sʲɪngas]
fragile (china, glass)	trapus	[tra'pʊs]
free (at no cost)	nemokamas	[nʲɛ'mokamas]

fresh (~ water)	gėlas	['gʲeːlʲas]
frozen (food)	užšáldytas	[ʊʒ'ʃalʲdʲiːtas]
full (completely filled)	pìlnas	['pʲɪlʲnas]
happy (adj)	laimìngas	[lʲʌɪ'mʲɪngas]
hard (not soft)	kíetas	['kʲiɛtas]
huge (adj)	vienódas	[vʲiɛ'nodas]
ill (sick, unwell)	sergantis	['sʲɛrgantʲɪs]
immobile (adj)	nėjudantis	['nʲɛjʊdantʲɪs]
important (adj)	svarbùs	[svar'bʊs]
interior (adj)	vidìnis	[vʲɪ'dʲɪnʲɪs]
last (e.g., ~ week)	praėjęs	[pra'eːjɛːs]
last (final)	paskutìnis	[paskʊ'tʲɪnʲɪs]
left (e.g., ~ side)	kairỹs	[kʌɪ'rʲiːs]
legal (legitimate)	teisėtas	[tʲɛɪ'sʲeːtas]
light (in weight)	leñgvas	['lʲɛngvas]
liquid (fluid)	skýstas	['skʲiːstas]
long (e.g., ~ hair)	ìlgas	['ɪlʲgas]
loud (voice, etc.)	stiprùs	[stʲɪp'rʊs]
low (voice)	tylùs	[tʲiː'lʲʊs]

27. Modifiers. Adjectives. Part 2

main (principal)	svarbùs	[svar'bʊs]
matt, matte	mãtinis	['maːtʲɪnʲɪs]
mysterious (adj)	paslaptìngas	[paslʲap'tʲɪngas]
narrow (street, etc.)	siaũras	['sʲɛuras]
native (~ country)	gìmtas	['gʲɪmtas]
negative (~ response)	neĩgiamas	['nʲɛɪgʲɛmas]
new (adj)	naũjas	['nɑujas]
next (e.g., ~ week)	tolèsnis	[to'lʲɛsnʲɪs]
normal (adj)	normalùs	[norma'lʲʊs]
not difficult (adj)	nesunkùs	[nʲɛsʊŋ'kʊs]
obligatory (adj)	privãlomas	[prʲɪ'vaːlʲomas]
old (house)	sẽnas	['sʲænas]
open (adj)	atidarýtas	[atʲɪda'rʲiːtas]
opposite (adj)	príešingas	['prʲiɛʃɪngas]
ordinary (usual)	pàprastas	['paprastas]
original (unusual)	originalùs	[orʲɪgʲɪna'lʲʊs]
personal (adj)	privatùs	[prʲɪva'tʊs]
polite (adj)	mandagùs	[manda'gʊs]
poor (not rich)	skurdùs	[skʊr'dʊs]
possible (adj)	įmãnomas	[iː'maːnomas]
principal (main)	pagrindìnis	[pagrʲɪn'dʲɪnʲɪs]

probable (adj)	tikétinas	[tɪ'kʲeːtʲɪnas]
prolonged (e.g., ~ applause)	ilgalaĩkis	[ɪlʲga'lʌɪkʲɪs]
public (open to all)	visuomenìnis	[vʲɪsʊɑmʲɛ'nʲɪnʲɪs]

rare (adj)	rētas	['rʲætas]
raw (uncooked)	žãlias	['ʒa:lʲæs]
right (not left)	dešinỹs	[dʲɛʃɪ'nʲiːs]
ripe (fruit)	prisĩrpęs	[prʲɪ'sʲɪrpʲɛːs]

risky (adj)	rizikìngas	[rʲɪzʲɪ'kʲɪngas]
sad (~ look)	liũdnas	['lʲuːdnas]
second hand (adj)	naudótas	[nɑʊ'dotas]
shallow (water)	seklùs	[sʲɛk'lʲʊs]
sharp (blade, etc.)	aštrùs	[aʃt'rʊs]

short (in length)	trum̃pas	['trʊmpas]
similar (adj)	panašùs	[pana'ʃʊs]
small (in size)	mãžas	['ma:ʒas]
smooth (surface)	lýgus	['lʲiːgʊs]
soft (~ toys)	mìnkštas	['mʲɪnkʃtas]

solid (~ wall)	patvarùs	[patva'rʊs]
sour (flavor, taste)	rūgštùs	[ru:gʃ'tʊs]
spacious (house, etc.)	erdvùs	[ɛrd'vʊs]
special (adj)	specialùs	[spʲɛtsʲɪja'lʲʊs]

straight (line, road)	tiesùs	[tʲiɛ'sʊs]
strong (person)	stiprùs	[stʲɪp'rʊs]
stupid (foolish)	kvaĩlas	['kvʌɪlʲas]
superb, perfect (adj)	puikùs	[pʊi'kʊs]

sweet (sugary)	saldùs	[salʲ'dʊs]
tan (adj)	įdẽgęs	[i:'dʲæɡʲɛːs]
tasty (delicious)	skanùs	[ska'nʊs]
unclear (adj)	neaĩškus	[nʲɛ'ʌɪʃkʊs]

28. Verbs. Part 1

to accuse (vt)	káltinti	['kalʲtʲɪntʲɪ]
to agree (say yes)	sutìkti	[sʊ'tʲɪktʲɪ]
to announce (vt)	paskélbti	[pas'kʲɛlʲptʲɪ]
to answer (vi, vt)	atsakýti	[atsa'kʲiːtʲɪ]
to apologize (vi)	atsiprašinéti	[atsʲɪpraʃɪ'nʲeːtʲɪ]

to arrive (vi)	atvažiúoti	[atva'ʒʲʊɑtʲɪ]
to ask (~ oneself)	kláusti	['klʲɑʊstʲɪ]
to be absent	nebúti	[nʲɛ'bu:tʲɪ]
to be afraid	bijóti	[bʲɪ'jotʲɪ]
to be born	gìmti	['gʲɪmtʲɪ]

to be in a hurry	skubėti	[skʊ'bʲe:tʲɪ]
to beat (to hit)	mušti	['mʊʃtʲɪ]
to begin (vt)	pradėti	[pra'dʲe:tʲɪ]
to believe (in God)	tikėti	[tʲɪ'kʲe:tʲɪ]
to belong to ...	priklausyti	[prʲɪklʲaʊ's'i:tʲɪ]
to break (split into pieces)	laužyti	['lʲaʊʒʲi:tʲɪ]

to build (vt)	statyti	[sta'tʲi:tʲɪ]
to buy (purchase)	pirkti	['pʲɪrktʲɪ]
can (v aux)	galėti	[ga'lʲe:tʲɪ]
can (v aux)	galėti	[ga'lʲe:tʲɪ]
to cancel (call off)	atšaukti	[at'ʃaʊktʲɪ]

to catch (vt)	gaudyti	['gaʊdʲi:tʲɪ]
to change (vt)	pakeisti	[pa'kʲɛɪstʲɪ]
to check (to examine)	tikrinti	['tʲɪkrʲɪntʲɪ]
to choose (select)	išsirinkti	[ɪʃsʲɪ'rʲɪŋktʲɪ]
to clean up (tidy)	tvarkyti	[tvar'kʲi:tʲɪ]

to close (vt)	uždaryti	[ʊʒda'rʲi:tʲɪ]
to compare (vt)	lyginti	['lʲi:gʲɪntʲɪ]
to complain (vi, vt)	skųstis	['sku:stʲɪs]

| to confirm (vt) | patvirtinti | [pat'vʲɪrtʲɪntʲɪ] |
| to congratulate (vt) | sveikinti | ['svʲɛɪkʲɪntʲɪ] |

to cook (dinner)	gaminti	[ga'mʲɪntʲɪ]
to copy (vt)	nukopijuoti	[nʊkopʲɪ'jʊatʲɪ]
to cost (vt)	kainuoti	[kʌɪ'nʊatʲɪ]

| to count (add up) | skaičiuoti | [skʌɪ'tʃʲʊatʲɪ] |
| to count on ... | tikėtis ... | [tʲɪ'kʲe:tʲɪs ...] |

to create (vt)	sukurti	[sʊ'kʊrtʲɪ]
to cry (weep)	verkti	['vʲɛrktʲɪ]
to dance (vi, vt)	šokti	['ʃoktʲɪ]

| to deceive (vi, vt) | apgaudinėti | [apgaʊdʲɪ'nʲe:tʲɪ] |
| to decide (~ to do sth) | spręsti | ['sprʲe:stʲɪ] |

to delete (vt)	ištrinti	[ɪʃ'trʲɪntʲɪ]
to demand (request firmly)	reikalauti	[rʲɛɪka'lʲaʊtʲɪ]
to deny (vt)	neigti	[nʲɛɪk'tʲɪ]

| to depend on ... | priklausyti nuõ ... | [prʲɪklʲaʊ's'i:tʲɪ nʊa ...] |
| to despise (vt) | smerkti | ['smʲɛrktʲɪ] |

to die (vi)	mirti	['mʲɪrtʲɪ]
to dig (vt)	rausti	['raʊstʲɪ]
to disappear (vi)	dingti	['dʲɪŋktʲɪ]
to discuss (vt)	aptarinėti	[aptarʲɪ'nʲætʲɪ]
to disturb (vt)	trukdyti	[trʊk'dʲi:tʲɪ]

29. Verbs. Part 2

to dive (vi)	nárdyti	['nardʲiːtʲɪ]
to divorce (vi)	išsiskìrti	[ɪʃsʲɪ'skʲɪrtʲɪ]
to do (vt)	darýti	[da'rʲiːtʲɪ]
to doubt (have doubts)	abejóti	[abʲɛ'jɔtʲɪ]
to drink (vi, vt)	gérti	['gʲɛrtʲɪ]

to drop (let fall)	numèsti	[nʊ'mʲɛstʲɪ]
to dry (clothes, hair)	džiovìnti	[dʒʲo'vʲɪntʲɪ]
to eat (vi, vt)	válgyti	['valʲgʲiːtʲɪ]
to end (~ a relationship)	nutráukti	[nʊ'traʊktʲɪ]
to excuse (forgive)	atléisti	[at'lʲɛɪstʲɪ]

to exist (vi)	egzistúoti	[ɛgzʲɪs'tʊatʲɪ]
to expect (foresee)	numatýti	[nʊma'tʲiːtʲɪ]
to explain (vt)	paáiškinti	[pa'ʌʃkʲɪntʲɪ]
to fall (vi)	krìsti	['krʲɪstʲɪ]
to fight (street fight, etc.)	mùštis	['mʊʃtʲɪs]
to find (vt)	ràsti	['rastʲɪ]

to finish (vt)	užbaìgti	[ʊʒ'bʌɪktʲɪ]
to fly (vi)	skrìsti	['skrʲɪstʲɪ]
to forbid (vt)	uždraũsti	[ʊʒ'draʊstʲɪ]
to forget (vi, vt)	užmìršti	[ʊʒ'mʲɪrʃtʲɪ]
to forgive (vt)	atléisti	[at'lʲɛɪstʲɪ]

to get tired	pavárgti	[pa'varktʲɪ]
to give (vt)	dúoti	['dʊatʲɪ]
to go (on foot)	eìti	['ɛɪtʲɪ]
to hate (vt)	nekẽsti	[nʲɛ'kʲɛːstʲɪ]

to have (vt)	turéti	[tʊ'rʲeːtʲɪ]
to have breakfast	pùsryčiauti	['pʊsrʲiːtʃɛʊtʲɪ]
to have dinner	vakarieniáuti	[vakarʲɪɛ'nʲæʊtʲɪ]
to have lunch	pietáuti	[pʲɪɛ'taʊtʲɪ]

to hear (vt)	girdéti	[gʲɪr'dʲeːtʲɪ]
to help (vt)	padéti	[pa'dʲeːtʲɪ]
to hide (vt)	slépti	['slʲeːptʲɪ]
to hope (vi, vt)	tikétis	[tʲɪ'kʲeːtʲɪs]
to hunt (vi, vt)	medžióti	[mʲɛ'dʒʲotʲɪ]
to hurry (vi)	skubéti	[skʊ'bʲeːtʲɪ]

to insist (vi, vt)	reikaláuti	[rʲɛɪka'lʲaʊtʲɪ]
to insult (vt)	įžeidinéti	[iːʒʲɛɪdʲɪ'nʲeːtʲɪ]
to invite (vt)	kviẽsti	['kvʲɛstʲɪ]
to joke (vi)	juokáuti	[jʊa'kaʊtʲɪ]
to keep (vt)	sáugoti	['saʊgotʲɪ]
to kill (vt)	žudýti	[ʒʊ'dʲiːtʲɪ]
to know (sb)	pažinóti	[paʒʲɪ'notʲɪ]

to know (sth)	žinóti	[ʒɪˈnotʲɪ]
to like (I like ...)	patìkti	[paˈtʲɪktʲɪ]
to look at ...	žiūréti į̇ ...	[ʒʲuːˈrʲeːtʲɪ iː ..]

to lose (umbrella, etc.)	pamèsti	[paˈmʲɛstʲɪ]
to love (sb)	myléti	[mʲiːˈlʲeːtʲɪ]
to make a mistake	klýsti	[ˈklʲiːstʲɪ]
to meet (vi, vt)	susitikinéti	[susʲɪtʲɪkʲɪˈnʲeːtʲɪ]
to miss (school, etc.)	praleidinéti	[pralʲɛɪdʲɪˈnʲeːtʲɪ]

30. Verbs. Part 3

to obey (vi, vt)	paklùsti	[pakˈlʲustʲɪ]
to open (vt)	atidarýti	[atʲɪdaˈrʲiːtʲɪ]
to participate (vi)	dalyváuti	[dalʲiːˈvɑutʲɪ]
to pay (vi, vt)	mokéti	[moˈkʲeːtʲɪ]
to permit (vt)	léisti	[ˈlʲɛɪstʲɪ]

to play (children)	žaìsti	[ˈʒɑɪstʲɪ]
to pray (vi, vt)	mèlstis	[ˈmʲɛlʲstʲɪs]
to promise (vt)	žadéti	[ʒaˈdʲeːtʲɪ]
to propose (vt)	siū́lyti	[ˈsʲuːlʲiːtʲɪ]
to prove (vt)	įródyti	[iːˈrodʲɪtʲɪ]
to read (vi, vt)	skaitýti	[skʌɪˈtʲiːtʲɪ]

to receive (vt)	gáuti	[ˈgɑutʲɪ]
to rent (sth from sb)	núomotis	[ˈnuɑmotʲɪs]
to repeat (say again)	kartóti	[karˈtotʲɪ]
to reserve, to book	rezervúoti	[rʲɛzʲɛrˈvuɑtʲɪ]
to run (vi)	bégti	[ˈbʲeːktʲɪ]

to save (rescue)	gélbéti	[ˈgʲælʲbʲeːtʲɪ]
to say (~ thank you)	pasakýti	[pasaˈkʲiːtʲɪ]
to see (vt)	matýti	[maˈtʲiːtʲɪ]
to sell (vt)	pardavinéti	[pardavʲɪˈnʲeːtʲɪ]
to send (vt)	išsiū́sti	[ɪʃˈsʲuːstʲɪ]
to shoot (vi)	šáudyti	[ˈʃɑudʲiːtʲɪ]

to shout (vi)	šaũkti	[ˈʃɑuktʲɪ]
to show (vt)	ródyti	[ˈrodʲiːtʲɪ]
to sign (document)	pasirašinéti	[pasʲɪraʃɪˈnʲeːtʲɪ]
to sing (vi)	dainúoti, giedóti	[dʌɪˈnuɑtʲɪ], [gʲiɛˈdotʲɪ]
to sit down (vi)	séstis	[ˈsʲeːstʲɪs]

to smile (vi)	šypsótis	[ʃʲɪːpˈsotʲɪs]
to speak (vi, vt)	sakýti	[saˈkʲiːtʲɪ]
to steal (money, etc.)	võgti	[ˈvoːktʲɪ]
to stop (please ~ calling me)	nustóti	[nuˈstotʲɪ]
to study (vt)	studijúoti	[studʲɪˈjuɑtʲɪ]

to swim (vi)	plaũkti	['plʲaʊktʲɪ]
to take (vt)	im̃ti	['ɪmtʲɪ]
to talk to …	kalbéti sù …	[kalʲˈbʲeːtʲɪ 'sʊ …]
to tell (story, joke)	pãsakoti	['pɑːsakotʲɪ]
to thank (vt)	dėko̅ti	[dʲeːˈkotʲɪ]
to think (vi, vt)	galvo̅ti	[galʲˈvotʲɪ]

to translate (vt)	veřsti	['vʲɛrstʲɪ]
to trust (vt)	pasitikéti	[pasʲɪtʲɪˈkʲeːtʲɪ]
to try (attempt)	bandýti	[ban'dʲiːtʲɪ]
to turn (e.g., ~ left)	sùkti	['sʊktʲɪ]
to turn off	išjùngti	[ɪˈʃjʊŋktʲɪ]

to turn on	įjùngti	[iːˈjʊŋktʲɪ]
to understand (vt)	suprãsti	[sʊpˈrastʲɪ]
to wait (vt)	láukti	['lʲaʊktʲɪ]
to want (wish, desire)	noréti	[noˈrʲeːtʲɪ]
to work (vi)	dìrbti	['dʲɪrptʲɪ]
to write (vt)	rašýti	[raˈʃiːtʲɪ]

www.ingramcontent.com/pod-product-compliance
Lightning Source LLC
Chambersburg PA
CBHW060026050426
42448CB00012B/2875